MY WORLD – AND WELCOME TO IT

"We're going through!" The Commander's voice was like thin ice breaking. He wore his full-dress uniform, with the heavily braided white cap pulled rakishly over one cold gray eye. "We can't make it, sir. It's spoiling for a hurricane, if you ask me." "I'm not asking you, Lieutenant Berg," said the Commander. "Throw on the power lights! Rev her up to 8,500! We're going through!" The pounding of the cylinders increased: ta-pocketa-pocketa-pocketa-*pocketa-pocketa*. The Commander stared at the ice forming on the pilot window. He walked over and twisted a row of complicated dials. "Switch on No. 8 auxiliary!" he shouted. "Switch on No. 8 auxiliary!" repeated Lieutenant Berg. "Full strength to No. 3 turret!" shouted the Commander. "Full strength in No. 3 turret!" The crew, bending to their various tasks in the huge, hurtling eight-engined Navy hydroplane, looked at each other and grinned. "The Old Man'll get us through," they said to one another. "The Old Man ain't afraid of Hell!". . .

"Not so fast! You're driving too fast!" said Mrs Mitty. "What are you driving so fast for?"

"Hmm?" said Walter Mitty.

James Thurber

MY WORLD –
AND WELCOME TO IT

With drawings by the author

A METHUEN PAPERBACK

First published in Great Britain in 1942
by Hamish Hamilton

This paperback edition published in 1987
by Methuen London Ltd
11 New Fetter Lane, London EC4P 4EE

Made and printed in Finland by Werner Söderström Oy

FOR NORMA AND ELLIOTT NUGENT

CONTENTS

Part One

Part Two

Part One

1

THE SECRET LIFE OF WALTER MITTY

"We're going through!" The Commander's voice was like thin ice breaking. He wore his full-dress uniform, with the heavily braided white cap pulled down rakishly over one cold gray eye. "We can't make it, sir. It's spoiling for a hurricane, if you ask me." "I'm not asking you, Lieutenant Berg," said the Commander. "Throw on the power lights! Rev her up to 8,500! We're going through!" The pounding of the cylinders increased: ta-pocketa-pocketa-pocketa-*pocketa-pocketa*. The Commander stared at the ice forming on the pilot window. He walked over and twisted a row of complicated dials. "Switch on No. 8 auxiliary!" he shouted. "Switch on No. 8 auxiliary!" repeated Lieutenant Berg. "Full strength to No. 3 turret!" shouted the Commander. "Full strength in No. 3 turret!" The crew, bending to their various tasks in the huge, hurtling eight-engined Navy hydroplane, looked at each other and grinned. "The Old Man'll get us through," they said to one another. "The Old Man ain't afraid of

Hell!" . . .

"Not so fast! You're driving too fast!" said Mrs. Mitty. "What are you driving so fast for?"

"Hmm?" said Walter Mitty. He looked at his wife, in the seat beside him, with shocked astonishment. She seemed grossly unfamiliar, like a strange woman who had yelled at him in a crowd. "You were up to fifty-five," she said. "You know I don't like to go more than forty. You were up to fifty-five." Walter Mitty drove on toward Waterbury in silence, the roaring of the SN202 through the worst storm in twenty years of Navy flying fading in the remote, intimate airways of his mind. "You're tensed up again," said Mrs. Mitty. "It's one of your days. I wish you'd let Dr. Renshaw look you over."

Walter Mitty stopped the car in front of the building where his wife went to have her hair done. "Remember to get those overshoes while I'm having my hair done," she said. "I don't need overshoes," said Mitty. She put her mirror back into her bag. "We've been all through that," she said, getting out of the car. "You're not a young man any longer." He raced the engine a little. "Why don't you wear your gloves? Have you lost your gloves?" Walter Mitty reached in a pocket and brought out the gloves. He put them on, but after she had turned and gone into the building and he had driven on to a red light, he took them off again. "Pick it up, brother!" snapped a cop as the light changed, and Mitty hastily pulled on his gloves and lurched ahead. He drove around the streets aimlessly for a time, and then he drove past the hospital on his way to the parking lot.

. . . "It's the millionaire banker, Wellington McMillan," said the pretty nurse. "Yes?" said Walter Mitty, removing his gloves slowly. "Who has the case?" "Dr. Renshaw and Dr. Benbow, but there are two specialists here, Dr. Remington from New York and Mr. Pritchard-Mitford from London. He flew over." A door opened down a long, cool corridor and Dr. Renshaw came out. He looked distraught and haggard. "Hello, Mitty," he said. "We're having the devil's own time with McMillan, the millionaire banker and close personal friend of Roosevelt. Obstreosis of the ductal tract. Tertiary. Wish you'd take a look at him." "Glad to," said Mitty.

In the operating room there were whispered introductions: "Dr. Remington, Dr. Mitty. Mr. Pritchard-Mitford, Dr. Mitty." "I've read your book on streptothricosis," said Pritchard-Mitford, shaking hands. "A brilliant performance, sir." "Thank you," said Walter Mitty. "Didn't know you were in the States, Mitty," grumbled Remington. "Coals to Newcastle, bringing Mitford and me up here for a tertiary." "You are very kind," said Mitty. A huge, complicated machine, connected to the operating table, with many tubes and wires, began at this moment to go pocketa-pocketa-pocketa. "The new anesthetizer is giving way!" shouted an interne. "There is no one in the East who knows how to fix it!" "Quiet, man!" said Mitty, in a low, cool voice. He sprang to the machine, which was now going pocketa-pocketa-queep-pocketa-queep. He began fingering delicately a row of glistening dials. "Give me a fountain pen!" he snapped. Someone handed him a fountain pen. He pulled a faulty piston out of the machine and inserted the pen in its place. "That will hold for ten minutes," he said. "Get on with the operation." A nurse hurried over and whispered to Renshaw, and Mitty saw the man turn pale. "Coreopsis has set in," said Renshaw nervously. "If you would take over, Mitty?" Mitty looked at him and at the craven figure of Benbow, who drank, and at the grave, uncertain faces of the two great specialists. "If you wish," he said. They slipped a white gown on him; he adjusted a mask and drew on thin gloves; nurses handed him shining . . .

"Back it up, Mac! Look out for that Buick!" Walter Mitty jammed on the brakes. "Wrong lane, Mac," said the parking-lot attendant, looking at Mitty closely. "Gee. Yeh," muttered Mitty. He began cautiously to back out of the lane marked "Exit Only." "Leave her sit there," said the attendant. "I'll put her away." Mitty got out of the car. "Hey, better leave the key." "Oh," said Mitty, handing the man the ignition key. The attendant vaulted into the car, backed it up with insolent skill, and put it where it belonged.

They're so damn cocky, thought Walter Mitty, walking along Main Street; they think they know everything. Once he had tried to take his chains off, outside New Milford, and he had got them wound around the axles. A man had had to come out in a wrecking car and unwind them, a young, grinning garageman. Since then Mrs. Mitty always made him drive to a garage to have the chains taken off. The next time, he thought, I'll wear my right arm in a sling; they won't grin at me then. I'll have my right arm in a sling and they'll see I couldn't possibly take the chains off myself. He kicked at the slush on the sidewalk. "Overshoes," he said to himself, and he began looking for a shoe store.

When he came out into the street again, with the overshoes in a box under his arm, Walter Mitty began to wonder what the other thing was his wife had told him to get. She had told him, twice, before they set out from their house for Waterbury. In a way he hated these weekly trips to town – he was always getting something wrong. Kleenex, he thought, Squibb's, razor blades? No. Toothpaste, toothbrush, bicarbonate, carborundum, initiative and referendum? He gave it up. But she would remember it. "Where's the what's-its-name?" she would ask. "Don't tell me you forgot the what's-its-name." A newsboy went by shouting something about the Waterbury trial.

. . . "Perhaps this will refresh your memory." The District Attorney suddenly thrust a heavy automatic at the quiet figure on the witness stand. "Have you ever seen this before?" Walter Mitty took the gun and examined it expertly. "This is my Webley-Vickers 50.80," he said calmly. An excited buzz ran around the courtroom. The Judge rapped for order. "You are a crack shot with any sort of firearms, I believe?" said the District Attorney, insinuatingly. "Objection!" shouted Mitty's attorney. "We have shown that the defendant could not have fired the shot. We have shown that he wore his right arm in a sling on the night of the fourteenth of July." Walter Mitty raised his hand briefly and the bickering attorneys were stilled. "With any known make of gun," he said evenly, "I could have killed Gregory Fitzhurst at three hundred feet *with my left hand*." Pandemonium broke loose in the courtroom. A woman's scream rose above the bedlam and suddenly a lovely, dark-haired girl was in Walter Mitty's arms. The District Attorney struck at her savagely. Without rising from his chair, Mitty let the man have it on the point of the chin. "You miserable cur!" . . .

"Puppy biscuit," said Walter Mitty. He stopped walking and the buildings of Waterbury rose up out of the misty courtroom and surrounded him again. A woman who was passing laughed. "He said 'Puppy biscuit', " she said to her companion. "That man said 'Puppy biscuit' to himself." Walter Mitty hurried on. He went into an A. & P., not the first one he came to but a smaller one farther up the street. "I want some biscuit for small, young dogs," he said to the clerk. "Any special brand, sir?" The greatest pistol shot in the world thought a moment. "It says 'Puppies Bark for It' on the box," said Walter Mitty.

His wife would be through at the hairdresser's in fifteen minutes, Mitty saw in looking at his watch, unless they had trouble drying it; sometimes they had trouble drying it. She didn't like to get to the hotel first; she would want him to be there waiting for her as usual. He found a big leather chair in the lobby, facing a window, and he put the overshoes and the puppy biscuit on the floor beside it. He picked up an old copy of *Liberty* and sank down into the chair. "Can Germany Conquer the World Through the Air?" Walter Mitty looked at the pictures of bombing planes and of ruined streets.

. . . "The cannonading has got the wind up in young

Raleigh, sir," said the sergeant. Captain Mitty looked up at him through touseled hair. "Get him to bed," he said wearily. "With the others. I'll fly alone." "But you can't, sir," said the sergeant anxiously. "It takes two men to handle that bomber and the Archies are pounding hell out of the air. Von Richtman's circus is between here and Saulier." "Somebody's got to get that ammunition dump," said Mitty. "I'm going over. Spot of brandy?" He poured a drink for the sergeant and one for himself. War thundered and whined around the dugout and battered at the door. There was a rending of wood and splinters flew through the room. "A bit of a near thing," said Captain Mitty carelessly. "The box barrage is closing in," said the sergeant. "We only live once, Sergeant," said Mitty, with his faint, fleeting smile. "Or do we?" He poured another brandy and tossed it off. "I never see a man could hold his brandy like you, sir," said the sergeant. "Begging your pardon, sir." Captain Mitty stood up and strapped on his huge Webley-Vickers automatic. "It's forty kilometres through hell, sir," said the sergeant. Mitty finished one last brandy. "After all," he said softly, "What isn't?" The pounding of the cannon increased; there was the rat-tat-tatting of machine guns, and from somewhere came the menacing pocketa-pocketa-pocketa of the new flame-throwers. Walter Mitty walked to the door of the dugout humming "Auprès de Ma Blonde." He turned and waved to the sergeant. "Cheerio!" he said . . . .

Something struck his shoulder. "I've been looking all over this hotel for you," said Mrs. Mitty. "Why do you have to hide in this old chair? How did you expect me to find you?" "Things close in," said Walter Mitty vaguely. "What?" Mrs. Mitty said. "Did you get the what's-its-name? The puppy biscuit? What's in that box?" "Over-shoes," said Mitty. "Couldn't you have put them on in the store?" "I was thinking," said Walter Mitty. "Does it ever occur to you that I am sometimes thinking?" She looked at him. "I'm going to take your temperature when I get you home," she said.

They went out through the revolving doors that made a faintly derisive whistling sound when you pushed them. It was two blocks to the parking lot. At the drugstore on the corner she said, "Wait here for me. I forgot something. I won't be a minute." She was more than a minute. Walter Mitty lighted a cigarette. It began to rain, rain with sleet in it. He stood up against the wall of the drugstore, smoking . . . He put his shoulders back and his heels together. "To hell with the handkerchief," said Walter Mitty scornfully. He took one last drag on his cigarette and snapped it away. Then, with that faint, fleeting smile playing about his lips, he faced the firing squad; erect and motionless, proud and disdainful, Walter Mitty the Unde-feated, inscrutable to the last.

2

COURTSHIP THROUGH THE AGES

Surely nothing in the astonishing scheme of life can have nonplussed Nature so much as the fact that none of the females of any of the species she created really cared very much for the male, as such. For the past ten million years Nature has been busily inventing ways to make the male attractive to the female, but the whole business of courtship, from the marine annelids up to man, still lumbers heavily along, like a complicated musical comedy. I have been reading the sad and absorbing story in Volume 6 (Cole to Dama) of the Encyclopaedia Britannica. In this volume you can learn all about cricket, cotton, costume designing, crocodiles, crown jewels, and Coleridge, but none of these subjects is so interesting as the Courtship of Animals, which recounts the sorrowful lengths to which all males must go to arouse the interest of a lady.

We all know, I think, that Nature gave man whiskers and a mustache with the quaint idea in mind that these would prove attractive to the female. We all know that, far from attracting her, whiskers and mustaches only made her nervous and gloomy, so that man had to go in for somersaults, tilting with lances, and performing feats and parlor magic to win her attention; he also had to bring her candy, flowers, and the furs of animals. It is common knowledge that in spite of all these "love displays" the male is constantly being turned down, insulted, or thrown out of the house. It is rather comforting, then, to discover that the peacock, for all his gorgeous plumage, does not have a particularly easy time in courtship; none of the males in the world do. The first peahen, it turned out, was only faintly stirred by her suitor's beautiful train. She would often go quietly to sleep while he was whisking it around. The Britannica tells us that the peacock actually had to learn a certain little trick to wake her up and revive her interest: he had to learn to vibrate his quills so as to make a rustling sound. In ancient times man himself, observing the ways of the peacock, probably tried vibrating his whiskers to make a rustling sound; if so, it didn't get him anywhere. He had to go in for something else; so, among other things, he went in for gifts. It is not unlikely that he got this idea from certain flies and birds who were making no headway at all with rustling sounds.

One of the flies of the family Empidae, who had tried everything, finally hit on something pretty special. He contrived to make a glistening transparent balloon which was even larger than himself. Into this he would put sweetmeats and tidbits and he would carry the whole elaborate envelope through the air to the lady of his choice. This amused her for a time, but she finally got bored with it. She demanded silly little colorful presents, something that you couldn't eat but that would look nice around the house. So the male Empis had to go around gathering flower petals and pieces of bright paper to put into his balloon. On a courtship flight a male Empis cuts quite a figure now, but he can hardly be said to be happy. He never knows how soon the female will demand heavier presents, such as Roman coins and gold collar buttons. It seems probable that one day the courtship of the Empidae will fall down, as man's occasionally does, of its own weight.

The bowerbird is another creature that spends so much time courting the female that he never gets any work done. If all the male bowerbirds became nervous wrecks within the next ten or fifteen years, it would not surprise me. The female bowerbird insists that a playground be built for her with a specially constructed bower at the entrance. This bower is much more elaborate than an ordinary nest and is harder to build; it costs a lot more, too. The female will not come to the playground until the male has filled it up with a great many gifts: silvery leaves, red leaves, rose petals, shells, beads, berries, bones, dice, buttons, cigar bands, Christmas seals, and the Lord knows what else. When the female finally condescends to visit the playground, she is in a coy and silly mood and has to be chased in and out of the bower and up and down the playground before she will quit giggling and stand still long enough even to shake hands. The male bird is, of course, pretty well done in before the chase starts, because he has worn himself out hunting for eyeglass lenses and begonia blossoms. I imagine that many a bowerbird, after chasing a female for two or three hours, says the hell with it and goes home to bed. Next day, of course, he telephones someone else and the same trying ritual is gone through with again. A male bowerbird is as exhausted as a night-club habitué before he is out of his twenties.

The male fiddler crab has a somewhat easier time, but it can hardly be said that he is sitting pretty. He has one enormously large and powerful claw, usually brilliantly colored, and you might suppose that all he had to do was reach out and grab some passing cutie. The very earliest fiddler crabs may have tried this, but, if so, they got slapped for their pains. A female fiddler crab will not tolerate any cave-man stuff; she never has and she doesn't intend to start now. To attract a female, a fiddler crab has to stand on tiptoe and brandish his claw in the air. If any female in the neighbourhood is interested – and you'd be surprised how many are not – she comes over and engages him in light badinage, for which he is not in the mood. As many as a hundred females may pass the time of day with him and go on about their business. By nightfall of an average courting day, a fiddler crab who has been standing on tiptoe for eight or ten hours waving a heavy claw in the air is in pretty sad shape. As in the case of the males of all species, however, he gets out of bed next morning, dashes some water on his face, and tries again.

The next time you encounter a male web-spinning spider, stop and reflect that he is too busy worrying about his love life to have any desire to bite you. Male web-spinning spiders have a tougher life than any other males in the animal kingdom. This is because the female web-spinning spiders have very poor eyesight. If a male lands on a female's web, she kills him before he has time to lay down his cane and gloves, mistaking him for a fly or a bumblebee who has stumbled into her trap. Before the species figured out what to do about this, millions of males were murdered by ladies they called on. It is the nature of spiders to perform a little dance in front of the female, but before a male spinner could get near enough for the female to see who he was and what he was up to, she would lash out at him with a flat-iron or a pair of garden shears. One night, nobody knows when, a very bright male spinner lay awake worrying about calling on a lady who had been killing suitors right and left. It came to him that this business of dancing as a love display wasn't getting anybody anywhere except the grave. He decided to go in for web-twitching, or strand-vibrating. The next day he tried it on one of the nearsighted girls. Instead of dropping in on her suddenly, he stayed outside the web and began monkeying with one of its strands. He twitched it up and down and in and out with such a lilting rhythm that the female was charmed. The serenade worked beautifully; the female let him live. The Britannica's spider-watchers, however, report that this system is not always success-ful. Once in a while, even now, a female will fire three bullets into a suitor or run him through with a kitchen knife. She keeps threatening him from the moment he strikes the first low notes on the outside strings, but usually by the time he has got up to the high notes played around the center of the web, he is going to town and she spares his life.

Even the butterfly, as handsome a fellow as he is, can't always win a mate merely by fluttering around and showing off. Many butterflies have to have scent scales on their wings. Hepialus carries a powder puff in a perfumed pouch. He throws perfume at the ladies when they pass. The male tree cricket, Oecanthus, goes Hepialus one better by carrying a tiny bottle of wine with him and giving drinks to such doxies as he has designs on. One of the male snails throws darts to entertain the girls. So it goes, through the long list of animals, from the bristle worm and his rudimentary dance steps to man and his gift of diamonds and sapphires. The golden-eye drake raises a jet of water with his feet as he flies over a lake; Hepialus has his powder puff, Oecanthus his wine bottle, man his etchings. It is a bright and melancholy story, the age-old desire of the male for the female, the age-old desire of the female to be amused and entertained. Of all the creatures on earth, the only males who could be figured as putting any irony into their courtship are the grebes and certain other diving birds. Every now and then a courting grebe slips quietly down to the bottom of a lake and then, with a mighty "Whoosh!," pops out suddenly a few feet from his girl friend, splashing water all over her. She seems to be persuaded that this is a purely loving display, but I like to think that the grebe always has a faint hope of drowning her or scaring her to death.

I will close this investigation into the mournful burdens of the male with the Britannica's story about a certain Argus pheasant. It appears that the Argus displays himself in front of a female who stands perfectly still without moving a feather. (If you saw "June Moon" some years ago and remember the scene in which the songwriter sang "Montana Moon" to his grim and motionless wife, you have some idea what the female Argus probably thinks of her mate's display.) The male Argus the Britannica tells about was confined in a cage with a female of another species, a female who kept moving around, emptying ashtrays and fussing with lampshades all the time the male was showing off his talents. Finally, in disgust, he stalked away and began displaying in front of his water trough. He reminds me of a certain male (Homo sapiens) of my acquaintance who one night after dinner asked his wife to put down her detective magazine so that he could read her a poem of which he was very fond. She sat quietly enough until he was well into the middle of the thing, intoning with great ardor and intensity. Then suddenly there came a sharp, disconcerting *slap!* It turned out that all during the male's display, the female had been intent on a circling mosquito and had finally trapped it between the palms of her hands. The male in this case did not stalk away and display in front of a water trough; he went over to Tim's and had a flock of drinks and recited the poem to the fellas. I am sure they all told bitter stories of their own about how their displays had been interrupted by females. I am also sure that they all ended up singing "Honey, Honey, Bless Your Heart."

3

THE WHIP-POOR-WILL

The night had just begun to get pale around the edges when the whip-poor-will began. Kinstrey, who slept in a back room on the first floor, facing the meadow and the strip of woods beyond, heard a blind man tapping and a bugle calling and a woman screaming "Help! Police!" The sergeant in gray was cutting open envelopes with a sword. "Sit down there, sit down there, sit down there!" he chanted at Kinstrey. "Sit down there, cut your throat, cut your throat, whip-poor-will, whip-poor-will, whip-poor-will!" And Kinstrey woke up.

He opened his eyes, but lay without moving for several minutes, separating the fantastic morning from the sounds and symbols of his dream. There was the palest wash of light in the room. Kinstrey scowled through tousled hair at his wristwatch and saw that it was ten minutes past four. "Whip-poor-will, whip-poor-will, whip-poor-will!" The bird sounded very near – in the grass outside the window, perhaps. Kinstrey got up and went to the window in his bare feet and looked out. You couldn't tell where the thing was. The sound was all around you, incredibly loud and compelling and penetrating. Kinstrey had never heard a whip-poor-will so near at hand before. He had heard them as a boy in Ohio in the country, but he remembered their call as faint and plaintive and faraway, dying before long somewhere between the hills and the horizon. You didn't hear the bird often in Ohio, it came back to him, and it almost never ventured as close to a house or barn as this brazen-breasted bird murdering sleep out there along the fence line somewhere. "Whip-poor-will, whip-poor-will, whip-poor-will!" Kinstrey climbed back into bed and began to count; the bird did twenty-seven whips without pausing. His lungs must be built like a pelican's pouch, or a puffin or a penguin or pemmican or a paladin . . . It was bright daylight when Kinstrey fell asleep again.

At breakfast, Madge Kinstrey, looking cool and well rested in her white piqué house coat, poured the coffee with steady authority. She raised her eyebrows slightly in mild surprise when Kinstrey mentioned the whip-poor-will the second time (she had not listened the first time, for she was lost in exploring with a long, sensitive finger an infinitesimal chip on the rim of her coffee cup).

"Whip-poor-will?" she said, finally. "No, I didn't hear it. Of course, my room is on the front of the house. You must have been slept out and ready to wake up anyway, or you wouldn't have heard it."

"Ready to wake up?" said Kinstrey. "At four o'clock in the morning? I hadn't slept three hours."

"Well, I didn't hear it," said Mrs Kinstrey. "I don't listen for night noises; I don't even hear the crickets or the frogs."

"Neither do I," said Kinstrey. "It's not the same thing. This thing is loud as a fire bell. You can hear it for a mile."

'I didn't hear it," she said, buttering a piece of thin toast.

Kinstrey gave it up and turned his scowling attention to the headlines in the *Herald Tribune* of the day before. The vision of his wife sleeping quietly in her canopied four-poster came between his eyes and the ominous headlines. Madge always slept quietly, almost without moving, her arms straight and still outside the covers, her fingers relaxed. She did not believe anyone had to toss and turn. "It's a notion," she would tell Kinstrey. "Don't let your nerves get the best of you. Use your will power."

"Um, hm," said Kinstrey aloud, not meaning to.

"Yes, sir?" said Arthur, the Kinstrey's colored butler, offering Kinstrey a plate of hot blueberry muffins.

"Nothing," said Kinstrey, looking at his wife. "Did you hear the whip-poor-will, Arthur?"

"No, sir, I didn't," said Arthur.

"Did Margaret?"

"I don't think she did, sir," said Arthur. "She didn't say anything about it."

The next morning the whip-poor-will began again at the same hour, rolling out its loops and circles of sound across the new day. Kinstrey, in his dreams, was beset by trios of little bearded men rolling hoops at him. He tried to climb up onto a gigantic Ferris wheel whose swinging seats were rumpled beds. The round cop with wheels for feet rolled toward him shouting, "Will power will, will power will, whip-poor-will!"

Kinstrey opened his eyes and stared at the ceiling and began to count the whips. At one point the bird did fifty-three straight, without pausing. I suppose, like the drops of water or the bright light in the third degree, this could drive you nuts, Kinstrey thought. Or make you confess. He began to think of things he hadn't thought of for years: the time he took the quarter from his mother's pocketbook, the time he steamed open a letter addressed to his father; it was from his teacher in the eighth grade. Miss – let's see – Miss Willpool, Miss Whippoor, Miss Will Power, Miss Wilmott – that was it.

He had reached the indiscretions of his middle twenties when the whip-poor-will suddenly stopped, on "poor," not on "will." Something must have frightened it. Kinstrey sat up on the edge of the bed and lighted a cigarette and listened. The bird was through calling, all right, but Kinstrey couldn't go back to sleep. The day was as bright as a flag. He got up and dressed.

"I thought you weren't going to smoke cigarettes before breakfast any more," said Madge later. "I found four stubs in the ashtray in your bedroom."

It was no use telling her he had smoked them before going to bed; you couldn't fool Madge; she always knew. "That goddam bird woke me up again," he said, "and this time I couldn't get back to sleep." He passed her his empty coffee cup. "It did fifty-three without stopping this morning," he added. "I don't know how the hell it breathes."

His wife took his coffee cup and set it down firmly. "Not three cups,' she said. "Not with you sleeping so restlessly the way it is."

"You didn't hear it, I suppose?" he said.

She poured herself some more coffee. "No," she said, "I didn't hear it."

Margaret hadn't heard it, either, but Arthur had. Kinstrey talked to them in the kitchen while they were clearing up after breakfast. Arthur said that it "Wuk" him but he went right back to sleep. He said he slept like a log – must be the air off the ocean. As for Margaret, she always slept like a log; only thing ever kept her awake was people a-hoopin' and a-hollerin'. She was glad she didn't hear the whip-poor-will. Down where she came from, she said, if you heard a whip-poor-will singing near the house, it meant there was going to be a death. Arthur said he had heard about that, too; must have been his grandma told him, or somebody.

If a whip-poor-will singing near the house meant death, Kinstrey told them, it wouldn't really make any difference whether you heard it or not. "It doesn't make any difference whether you see the ladder you're walking under," he said, lighting a cigarette and watching the effect of his words on Margaret. She turned from putting some plates away, and her eyes widened and rolled a little.

"Mr Kinstrey is just teasin' you, Mag," said Arthur, who smiled and was not afraid. Thinks he's pretty smart, Kinstrey thought. Just a little bit too smart, maybe.

Kinstrey remembered Arthur's way of smiling, almost imperceptibly, at things Mrs. Kinstrey sometimes said to her husband when Arthur was just coming into the room or just going out – little things that were none of his business to listen to. Like "Not three cups of coffee if a bird keeps you awake." Wasn't that what she had said?

"Is there any more coffee?" he asked, testily. "Or did you throw it out?" He knew they had thrown it out; breakfast had been over for almost an hour.

"We can make you some fresh," said Arthur.

"Never mind," said Kinstrey. "Just don't be so sure of yourself. There's nothing in life to be sure about."

When, later in the morning, he started out the gate to walk down to the post office, Madge called to him from an upstairs window. "Where are you going?" she asked, amiably enough. He frowned up at her. "To the taxidermist's," he said, and went on.

He realized, as he walked along in the warm sunlight, that he had made something of a spectacle of himself. Just because he hadn't had enough sleep – or enough coffee. It wasn't his fault, though. It was that infernal bird. He discovered, after a quarter of a mile, that the imperative rhythm of the whip-poor-will's call was running through his mind, but the words of the song were new: fatal bell, fatal bell, fa-tal bell. Now, where had that popped up from? It took him some time to place it; it was a fragment from "Macbeth." There was something about the fatal bellman crying in the night. "The fatal bellman cried the live-long night" – something like that. It was an owl that cried the night Duncan was murdered. Funny thing to call up after all these years; he hadn't read the play since college. It was that fool Margaret, talking about the whip-poor-will and the old superstition that if you hear the whip-poor-will singing near the house, it means there is going to be a death. Here it was 1942, and people still believed in stuff like that.

The next dawn the dream induced by the calling of the whip-poor-will was longer and more tortured – a nightmare filled with dark perils and heavy hopelessness. Kinstrey woke up trying to cry out. He lay there breathing hard and listening to the bird. He began to count: one, two, three, four, five . . .

Then, suddenly, he leaped out of bed and ran to the window and began yelling and pounding on the windowpane and running the blind up and down. He shouted and cursed until his voice got hoarse. The bird kept right on going. He slammed the window down and turned away from it, and there was Arthur in the doorway.

"What is it, Mr. Kinstrey?" said Arthur. He was fumbling with the end of a faded old bathrobe and trying to blink the sleep out of his eyes. "Is anything the matter?"

Kinstrey glared at him. "Get out of here!" he shouted. "And put some coffee on. Or get me a brandy or something."

"I'll put some coffee on," said Arthur. He went shuffling away in his slippers, still half asleep.

"Well," said Madge Kinstrey over her coffee cup at breakfast, "I hope you got your tantrum over and done

with this morning. I never heard such a spectacle –
squalling like a spoiled brat."

"You can't hear spectacles," said Kinstrey, coldly.
"You see them."

"I'm sure I don't know what you're talking about," she
said.

No, you don't, thought Kinstrey, you never have; never
have, nev-er have, nev-er have. Would he ever get that
damned rhythm out of his head? It struck him that
perhaps Madge had no subconscious. When she lay on her
back, her eyes closed; when she got up, they opened, like a
doll's. The mechanism of her mind was as simple as a
cigarette box; it was either open or it was closed, and there
was nothing else, nothing else, nothing else . . .

The whole problem turns on a very neat point, Kinstrey
thought as he lay awake that night, drumming on the
headboard with his fingers. William James would have
been interested in it; Henry, too, probably. I've got to
ignore this thing, get adjusted to it, become oblivious of it.
I mustn't fight it, I mustn't build it up. If I get to
screaming at it, I'll be running across that wet grass out
there in my bare feet, charging that bird as if it were a
trench full of Germans, throwing rocks at it, giving the
Rebel yell or something, for God's sake. No, I mustn't
build it up. I'll think of something else every time it pops
into my mind. I'll name the Dodger infield to myself, over
and over: Camilli, Herman, Reese, Vaughan, Camilli,
Herman, Reese . . .

Kinstrey did not succeed in becoming oblivious of the

whip-poor-will. Its dawn call pecked away at his dreams like a vulture at a heart. It slowly carved out a recurring nightmare in which Kinstrey was attacked by an umbrella whose handle, when you clutched it, clutched right back, for the umbrella was not an umbrella at all but a raven. Through the gloomy hallways of his mind rang the Thing's dolorous cry: nevermore, nevermore, nevermore, whip-poor-will, whip-poor-will . . .

One day, Kinstrey asked Mr. Tetford at the post office if the whip-poor-wills ever went away. Mr. Tetford squinted at him. "Don't look like the sun was brownin' you up none," he said. "I don't know as they ever go away. They move around. I like to hear 'em. You get used to 'em."

"Sure," said Kinstrey. "What do people do when they can't get used to them, though – I mean old ladies or sick people?"

"Only one's been bothered was old Miss Purdy. She darn near set fire to the whole island tryin' to burn 'em out of her woods. Shootin' at 'em might drive 'em off, or a body could trap 'em easy enough and let 'em loose somewheres else. But people get used to 'em after a few mornings."

"Oh, sure," said Kinstrey. "Sure."

That evening in the living room, when Arthur brought in the coffee, Kinstrey's cup cackled idiotically in its saucer when he took it off the tray.

Madge Kinstrey laughed. "Your hand is shaking like a leaf," she said.

He drank all his coffee at once and looked up savagely.

"If I could get one good night's sleep, it might help," he said. "That damn bird! I'd like to wring its neck."

"Oh, come, now," she said, mockingly. "You wouldn't hurt a fly. Remember the mouse we caught in the Westport house? You took it out in the field and let it go."

"The trouble with you – " he began, and stopped. He opened the lid of a cigarette box and shut it, opened and shut it again, reflectively. "As simple as that," he said.

She dropped her amused smile and spoke shortly. "You're acting like a child about that silly bird," she said. "Worse than a child. I was over at the Barrys' this afternoon. Even their little Ann didn't make such a fuss. A whip-poor-will frightened her the first morning, but now she never notices them."

"I'm not frightened, for God's sake!" shouted Kinstrey. "Frightened or brave, asleep or awake, open or shut – you make everything black or white."

"Well," she said, "I like that."

"I think the bird wakes you up, too," he said. "I think it wakes up Arthur and Margaret."

"And we just pretend it doesn't?" she asked. "Why on earth should we?"

"Oh, out of some fool notion of superiority, I suppose. Out of – I don't know."

"I'll thank you not to class me with the servants," she said coldly. He lighted a cigarette and didn't say anything. "You're being ridiculous and childish," she said, "fussing about nothing at all, like an invalid in a wheel chair." She got up and started from the room.

"Nothing at all," he said, watching her go.

She turned at the door. "Ted Barry says he'll take you on at tennis if your bird hasn't worn you down too much." She went on up the stairs, and he heard her close the door of her room.

He sat smoking moodily for a long time, and fell to wondering whether the man's wife in "The Raven" had seen what the man had seen perched on the pallid bust of Pallas just above the chamber door. Probably not, he decided. When he went to bed, he lay awake a long while trying to think of the last line of "The Raven." He couldn't get any farther than "Like a demon that is dreaming," and this kept running through his head. "Nuts," he said at last, aloud, and he had the oddly disturbing feeling that it wasn't he who had spoken but somebody else.

Kinstrey was not surprised that Madge was a little girl in pigtails and a play suit. The long gray hospital room was filled with poor men in will chairs, running their long, sensitive fingers around the rims of empty coffee cups. "Poor Will, poor Will," chanted Madge, pointing her finger at him. "Here are your spectacles, here are your spectacles." One of the sick men was Arthur, grinning at him, grinning at him and holding him with one hand, so that he was powerless to move his arms or legs. "Hurt a fly, hurt a fly," chanted Madge. "Whip him now, whip him now!" she cried, and she was the umpoor in the high chair beside the court, holding a black umbrella over her head: love thirty, love forty, forty-one, forty-two, forty-three, forty-four. His feet were stuck in the wet concrete on his side of the net and Margaret peered over the net at him, holding a skillet for a racquet. Arthur was pushing him down now, and he was caught in the concrete from head to foot. It was Madge laughing and counting over him: refer-three, refer-four, refer-five, refer-will, repoor-will, whip-poor-will, whip-poor-will, whip-poor-will . . .

The dream still clung to Kinstrey's mind like a cobweb as he stood in the kitchen in his pajamas and bare feet, wondering what he wanted, what he was looking for. He turned on the cold water in the sink and filled a glass, but only took a sip, and put it down. He left the water running. He opened the breadbox and took out half a loaf wrapped in oiled paper, and pulled open a drawer. He took out the bread knife and then put it back and took out the long, sharp carving knife. He was standing there holding the knife in one hand and the bread in the other when the door to the dining room opened. It was Arthur. "Who do you do first?" Kinstrey said to him, hoarsely. . . .

The Barrys, on their way to the beach in their station wagon, drove into the driveway between the house and the barn. They were surprised to see that, at a quarter to eleven in the morning, the Kinstrey servants hadn't taken in the milk. The bottle, standing on the small back porch, was hot to Barry's touch. When he couldn't rouse anyone, pounding and calling, he climbed up on the cellar door and looked in the kitchen window. He told his wife sharply to get back in the car. . . .

The local police and the state troopers were in and out of the house all day. It wasn't every morning in the year that you got called out on a triple murder and suicide.

It was just getting dark when Troopers Baird and Lennon came out of the front door and walked down to their car, pulled up beside the road in front of the house. Out in back, probably in the little strip of wood there, Lennon figured, a whip-poor-will began to call. Lennon listened a minute. "You ever hear the old people say a whip-poor-will singing near the house means death?" he asked.

Baird grunted and got in under the wheel. Lennon climbed in beside him. "Take more'n a whip-poor-will to cause a mess like that," said Trooper Baird, starting the car.

4

THE MACBETH MURDER MYSTERY

"It was a stupid mistake to make," said the American woman I had met at my hotel in the English lake country, "but it was on the counter with the other Penguin books – the little sixpenny ones, you know, with the paper covers – and I supposed of course it was a detective story. All the others were detective stories. I'd read all the others, so I bought this one without really looking at it carefully. You can imagine how mad I was when I found it was Shakespeare." I murmured something sympathetically. "I don't see why the Penguin-books people had to get out Shakespeare's plays in the same size and everything as the detective stories," went on my companion. "I think they have different-colored jackets," I said. "Well, I didn't notice that," she said. "Anyway, I got real comfy in bed that night and all ready to read a good mystery story and here I had 'The Tragedy of Macbeth' – a book for high-school students. Like 'Ivanhoe'." "Or 'Lorna Doone'," I said. "Exactly," said the American lady. "And I was just crazy for a good Agatha Christie, or something. Hercule Poirot is my favorite detective." "Is he the rabbity one?" I asked. "Oh, no," said my crime-fiction expert. "He's the Belgian one. You're thinking of Mr. Pinkerton, the one that helps Inspector Bull. He's good, too."

Over her second cup of tea my companion began to tell the plot of a detective story that had fooled her completely – it seems it was the old family doctor all the time. But I cut in on her. "Tell me," I said. "Did you read 'Macbeth'?" "*I had* to read it," she said. "There wasn't a scrap of anything else to read in the whole room." "Did you like it?" I asked. "No, I did not," she said, decisively. "In the first place, I don't think for a moment that Macbeth did it." I looked at her blankly. "Did what?" I asked. "I don't think for a moment that he killed the King," she said. "I don't think the Macbeth woman was mixed up in it, either. You suspect them the most, of course, but those are the ones that are never guilty – or shouldn't be, anyway." "I'm afraid," I began, "that I – " "But don't you see?" said the American lady. "It would spoil everything if you could figure out right away who did it. Shakespeare was too smart for that. I've read that people never *have* figured out 'Hamlet', so it isn't likely Shakespeare would have made 'Macbeth' as simple as it seems." I thought this over while I filled my pipe. "Who do you suspect?" I asked, suddenly. "Macduff," she said, promptly. "Good God!" I whispered, softly.

"Oh, Macduff did it, all right," said the murder specialist. "Hercule Poirot would have got him easily." "How did you figure it out?" I demanded. "Well," she said, "I didn't right away. At first I suspected Banquo. And then, of course, he was the second person killed. That was good right in there, that part. The person you suspect of the first murder should always be the second victim." "Is that so?" I murmured. "Oh, yes," said my informant. "They have to keep surprising you. Well, after the second murder I didn't know *who* the killer was for a while." "How about Malcolm and Donalbain, the King's sons?" I asked. "As I remember it, they fled right after the first murder. That looks suspicious." "Too suspicious," said the American lady. "Much too suspicious. When they flee, they're never guilty. You can count on that." "I believe," I said, "I'll have a brandy," and I summoned the waiter. My companion leaned toward me, her eyes bright, her teacup quivering. "Do you know who discovered Duncan's body?" she demanded. I said I was sorry, but I had forgotten. "Macduff discovers it," she said, slipping into the historical present. "Then he comes running downstairs and shouts, 'Confusion has broke ope the Lord's anointed temple' and 'Sacrilegious murder has made his masterpiece' and on and on like that." The good lady tapped me on the knee. "All that stuff was *rehearsed*," she said. "You wouldn't say a lot of stuff like that, offhand, would you – if you had found a body?" She fixed me with a glittering eye. "I – " I began. "You're right!" she said. "You wouldn't! Unless you had practised it in advance. 'My God, there's a body in here!' is what an innocent man would say." She sat back with a confident glare.

I thought for a while. "But what do you make of the Third Murderer?" I asked. "You know, the Third

Murderer has puzzled 'Macbeth' scholars for three hundred years." "That's because they never thought of Macduff," said the American lady. "It was Macduff, I'm certain. You couldn't have one of the victims murdered by two ordinary thugs – the murderer always has to be somebody important." "But what about the banquet scene?" I asked, after a moment. "How do you account for Macbeth's guilty actions there, when Banquo's ghost came in and sat in his chair?" The lady leaned forward and tapped me on the knee again. "There wasn't any ghost," she said. "A big, strong man like that doesn't go around seeing ghosts – especially in a brightly lighted banquet hall with dozens of people around. Macbeth was *shielding somebody!*" "Who was he shielding?" I asked. "Mrs. Macbeth, of course," she said. "He thought she did it and he was going to take the rap himself. The husband always does that when the wife is suspected." "But what," I demanded, "about the sleepwalking scene, then?" "The same thing, only the other way around," said my companion. "That time *she* was shielding *him*. She wasn't asleep at all. Do you remember where it says, 'Enter Lady Macbeth with a taper'?" "Yes," I said. "Well, people who walk in their sleep *never carry lights!*" said my fellow-traveller. "They have a second sight. Did you ever hear of a sleepwalker carrying a light?" "No," I said, "I never did." "Well, then, she wasn't asleep. She was acting guilty to shield Macbeth." "I think," I said, "I'll have another brandy," and I called the waiter. When he brought it, I drank it rapidly and rose to go. "I believe," I said, "that you have got hold of something. Would you lend me that

'Macbeth'? I'd like to look it over tonight. I don't feel, somehow, as if I'd ever really read it." "I'll get it for you," she said. "But you'll find that I am right."

I read the play over carefully that night, and the next morning, after breakfast, I sought out the American woman. She was on the putting green, and I came up behind her silently and took her arm. She gave an exclamation. "Could I see you alone?" I asked, in a low voice. She nodded cautiously and followed me to a secluded spot. "You've found out something?" she breathed. "I've found out," I said, triumphantly, "the name of the murderer!" "You mean it wasn't Macduff?" she said. "Macduff is as innocent of those murders," I said, "as Macbeth and the Macbeth woman." I opened the copy of the play, which I had with me, and turned to Act II, Scene 2. "Here," I said, "you will see where Lady Macbeth says, 'I laid their daggers ready. He could not miss 'em. Had he not resembled my father as he slept, I had done it.' Do you see?" "No," said the American woman, bluntly, "I don't." "But it's simple!" I exclaimed. "I wonder I didn't see it years ago. The reason Duncan resembled Lady Macbeth's father as he slept is that *it actually was her father*!" "Good God!" breathed my companion, softly. "Lady Macbeth's father killed the King," I said, "and, hearing someone coming, thrust the body under the bed and crawled into the bed himself." "But," said the lady, "you can't have a murderer who only appears in the story once. You can't have that." "I know that," I said, and I turned to Act II, Scene 4. "It says here,

'Enter Ross with an old Man.' Now, that old man is never identified and it is my contention he was old Mr. Macbeth, whose ambition it was to make his daughter Queen. There you have your motive." "But even then," cried the American lady, "he's still a minor character!" "Not," I said, gleefully, "when you realize that he was also *one of the weird sisters in disguise!*" "You mean one of the three witches?" "Precisely," I said. "Listen to this speech of the old man's. 'On Tuesday last, a falcon towering in her pride of place, was by a mousing owl hawk'd at and kill'd.' Who does that sound like?" "It sounds like the way the three witches talk," said my companion, reluctantly. "Precisely!" I said again. "Well," said the American woman, "maybe you're right, but – " "I'm sure I am," I said. "And do you know what I'm going to do now?" "No," she said. "What?" "Buy a copy of 'Hamlet'," I said, "and solve *that!*" My companion's eyes brightened. "Then," she said, "you don't think Hamlet did it?" "I am," I said, "absolutely positive he didn't." "But who," she demanded, "do you suspect?" I looked at her cryptically. "Everybody," I said, and disappeared into a small grove of trees as silently as I had come.

5

THE PREOCCUPATION OF
MR. PEFFIFOSS

In a time when everything should be made as simple and uncomplicated as possible, the Connecticut Telephone Company has taken to changing a lot of peaceful old rural phone numbers which had been doing all right the way they were. For several years I have known by heart the number of some friends of mine who live in a quiet little house out in the country, eight miles from town – New Milford 905 Ring 4, a pleasant number, easily remembered and easily spoken. When I called it the other day, I was told the number had been changed to New Milford 1006 W-1. New Milford One Oh Oh Six Double-U One.

Lots worse things have happened to me, but not many that I keep thinking about more often. I have slowly built up in my mind a picture of the official in Hartford who thought up that change. His name, as it comes to me in dreams, is Rudwooll Y. Peffifoss. Peffifoss, who has had to go through a lot of hell, not only on account of the name Peffifoss, but also on account of Rudwooll (the Y is for

Yurmurm), has had to compensate for what has happened to him in this life. Working up relentlessly and maliciously to an important post in the Number Changing Department of the Connecticut Telephone Company, he had decided to get back at the world for what he conceives it has done to him. He spends the day going through phone books looking for simple, easily remembered numbers, like 905 Ring 4, and when he finds one, he claps his hands and calls in his secretary, a Miss Rettig.

"Take a number change, Miss Rettig," he says with an evil smile. "New Milford 905 Ring 4 to be changed to Pussymeister W-7 Oh 8 Oh 9 6 J-4."

Miss Rettig, who has gone through this every day for months, sits patiently and waits for his fiendish glee to subside, and then reminds him, as she has to do a dozen times a day, that such a number is not yet possible under the company's regulations. She hastily adds that of course it will be possible when Mr. Peffifoss finally gets complete charge of the company.

Somewhat mollified, Peffifoss snarls for a while, but in the end agrees to stay within bounds. He writes down all the tough arrangements of authorized numbers he can think of and tries them out on Miss Rettig. When she stumbles several times trying to say New Milford One Oh Oh Six Double-U One, he claps his hands and okays the change. It hasn't been such a bad day after all, and Rudwooll Yurmurm Peffifoss goes home in what for him are high spirits, to kick his children's rabbits around a while before sitting down to dinner.

6

BACKWARD AND DOWNWARD WITH MR. PUNCH

Looking for a Roman coin I had dropped on the library floor of the house I rented for the winter, I found, on a shelf behind a sofa, two dozen immense bound volumes of *Punch*. They contained all the copies of the famous British weekly from the year it was founded until 1891, exactly half a century later. I picked out three volumes at random and began idly turning the pages of first one and then another. When the following Tuesday found me still at it, I realized what I was up to: I was getting ready to make some kind of report on Mr. Punch of the nineteenth century. If it has been done before, all I can say is that I am doing it again.

Let us begin, then, with the tome which contains the issues from July, 1889, to July, 1891, and work our way back toward the Civil War. This volume, like all the others, contains some rather heavy introductory notes summarizing what was going on in the world at the time. In this two-year period quite a lot was going on, if you have forgotten. The "young and impetuous" Kaiser Wilhelm was rattling his saber and already disturbing the peace of mind of Europe. The volume falls open easily at the double page containing Tenniel's famous cartoon "Dropping the Pilot" – for it was at this time that Wilhelm got rid of Bismarck. Socialism was raising its troublesome head, so terrifying Mr. Punch that he had Tenniel draw a cartoon of a serpent (Socialism) wrapped about the body of an eagle (Trade) and striving to crush the bird's wings (Capital and Labor). The brief, sad romance of Parnell and Captain O'Shea's wife shocked the British Isles and formed a dark foil for the decorous private life of Mr. Gladstone, who, past eighty years old, celebrated his golden-wedding anniversary. Tennyson, the poet laureate, became an octogenarian in his turn, and Browning died two years short of the mark. A potato famine was predicted in Ireland and an epidemic of influenza held the world in what I am sure *Punch*, somewhere or other, must have called its grip. A young pianist whom *Punch* laughingly alluded to as "Paddy Rewski from Irish Poland" gave a concert in London, but *Punch* could not appraise the young man's talents because *Punch* did not attend the concert. *Punch* could report, however, that the life in Marion Crawford's latest novel was real life and that Mr. Ibsen's "A Doll's House" was "unutterably loathsome" and should be removed from the stages of the world.

The harsh effects on the feminine complexion of that new invention, the electric light, gave *Punch* a hundred whimsical ideas, and so did the new and wonderful Eiffel Tower. (One proud London paper wrote, "The Eiffel

Tower is 1,000 feet high; the Forth bridge, if stood on end, would be 5,280 feet in height.") Mr. Edison's phonograph was received with proper respect, *Punch* calling up the spirit of Faraday, who solemnly approved of the device. Montana, the Dakotas, and Washington were admitted to the Union and the government breathed more easily when Sitting Bull was shot dead. Barnum was in London with his great show and Millet's "The Angelus" was sold to an American. A hydrophobia scare led to the muzzling of all the dogs in England and *Punch* came out for the much-abused Pasteur in a drawing with this dialogue between a husband and wife:

> "Oh, Joseph! Teddy's just been bitten by a strange dog! Doctor says we'd better take him over to Pasteur *at once!*"
> "But, my love, I've just written and published a violent attack upon M. Pasteur, on the score of his cruelty to rabbits! And at *your instigation*, too!"
> "Oh, Heavens! Never mind the rabbits *now!* What are all the rabbits in the world compared to *our only child?*"

Among the minor objects of Mr. Punch's annoyance during these years were Mr. Pinero for an attack on the London music halls, newfangled barbed wire fences for interfering with fox-hunting, the Americans for coining so much money and so many new words, and Count Tolstoi for a savage assault on tobacco smokers. Of this last *Punch* rhymed, in part:

> Tolstoi knew a man who said

> He cut off a woman's head;
> But, when half the deed was done,
> Lo, the murderer's courage gone!
> And he finished, 'tis no joke,
> Only by the aid of smoke.

Unhorrified by murderers who got a lift from nicotine, Mr. Punch could not approve of the use of the weed by ladies, some of whom were apparently going in for cigars:

> You're beautiful, but fairer far
> You'd be – if only you would let
> Your male friends smoke that big cigar
> And yield them, too, that cigarette.

Most of the jokes in this volume are about bad cooks, worse painters, errant nursemaids, precocious children, insolent cabdrivers, and nonchalant young blades in ballrooms. I found, somewhat to my surprise, that a great many of these young blades were named Gus. I found, also to my surprise, that the expression "I'm nuts on," meaning "I'm crazy about," was used in 1891. And that the Irate-Voice-from-Upstairs joke began fifty years ago (unless what I ran across was just a revival of it):

STERN VOICE (*from first-floor landing, temp. 12.10 p.m.*): Alice!

ALICE (*softly*): Yes, "Pa"!

VOICE (*with threatening ring in it*): Does that young man in the front parlor take tea or coffee for his breakf-!!?

(*"Door" – and he was gone!*)

During the eighties and nineties Mr. Henry James (of

whom I could find no mention anywhere in *Punch*) was in the midst of his elaborate and delicate examinations of American ladies abroad, but Mr. Punch lashed out at them in a simpler manner:

SIR JAMES: And were you in Rome?

AMERICAN LADY: I guess not. (*To her daughter.*) Say, Bella, did we visit Rome?

FAIR DAUGHTER: Why, Ma, certainly! Don't you remember? It was in Rome we bought the lisle-thread stockings!

(*American lady is convinced*)

The American male comes in for it, too:

YOUNG BRITISHER: Your father's not with you, then, Miss Van Tromp?

FAIR NEW YORK MILLIONAIRESS (*one of three*): Why, no – Pa's much too vulgar! It's as much as we can do to stand Ma!

Sometimes *Punch* had at our damsels in verse:

THE AMERICAN GIRL

She "guesses" and she "calculates", she wears all sorts o'
    collars,
  Her yellow hair is not without suspicion of a dye;
Her "páppa" is a dull old man who turned pork into dollars,
  But everyone admits that she's indubitably spry.

She did Rome in a swift two days, gave half the time to Venice,
  But vows that she saw everything, although in awful haste;
She's fond of dancing, but she seems to fight shy of lawn tennis,
  Because it might endanger the proportions of her waist.

Her manner might be well defined as elegantly skittish;
  She loves a Lord as only a Republican can do;
And quite the best of titles she's persuaded are the British,
  And well she knows the Peerage, for she's read it through and
    through.

She's bediamonded superbly and shines like a constellation,
  You scarce can see her fingers for the multitude of rings;
She's just a shade too conscious, as it seems, of admiration,
  With irritating tendencies to wriggle when she sings.

She owns she is "Amur'can," and her accent is alarming;
  Her birthplace is an awful name you pray you may forget;
Yet, after all, we own "La Belle Américaine" is charming,
  So let us hope she'll win at last her long-sought coronet.

Phil May, a great caricaturist, came back to London in the early nineties after a long stay in Australia, but his work does not appear in this volume. It could have used some. Before I leave this engrossing period of history and humor I must quote a typical Foreigner-in-the-English-Home joke. This one, with its evidence of the nineteenth-century Englishman's fine ear for the German accent, is my favorite of several hundred:

> HOSTESS: Won't you try some of that jelly, Herr Silbermund?
>
> HERR SILBERMUND (*who has just been helped to pudding*): Ach, zank you, no. I voot "rahzer pear viz ze ills ve haf zan vly to ozzers ve know not of".

In the years 1869 to 1871 (our second volume), Mr. Punch had a wealth of subjects for his little punning pieces and his big political posters. The Fenians in Ireland and

America were raising hell on behalf of the freedom of Erin, and the Alabama claims case was still a sore point between England and America. Harriet Beecher Stowe, having freed the slaves, nosed about in the private life of the late Lord Byron and provided the great scandal of the day in a magazine article revealing the love story of the poet and his half sister, Augusta Leigh. General Dan Sickles, hero of the Peach Orchard at Gettysburg, who was god-damming up and down the American chancellery in Madrid as our ambassador, informed his government that the Spaniards were sore about our friendly attitude toward the Cuban insurrectionists and might do something about it. On the eighteenth of July, 1870, the infallibility of the Pope was declared. On the next day France declared war on Prussia and rushed headlong to defeat, the French *mitrailleuse* proving less deadly than the Prussian needle gun. Disraeli published a novel called "Lothair" and made Bartlett's "Quotations" with a crack about critics being people who have failed in literature and the arts. Oxford beat Harvard in the first crew race ever rowed between the two universities and a small, resolute band of women began to clamor for the right to vote. Darwin's "The Descent of Man" was pie for the wits of *Punch*, and the magazine cried out against the deplorable fact that the word "reliable", which it described as "a new and unnecessary American adjective", was creeping into the inviolable English tongue. On top of everything the women of England were affecting the "Grecian bend", which *Punch* called "an exaggerated forward inclination of the body, an absurd fashion of the hour".

I devoted a great deal of my research to hunting down seventy-year-old versions of jokes which are still going the rounds, and I offer my most cherished discovery:

THE CURATE: O dear, O dear! Drunk again, Jones! *Drunk* again! And in broad daylight, too!

JONES: Lorsh (*hic*)! Whatsh the oddsh! Sh-Sh-Sho am *I*!

You will remember this one, too:

TICKET COLLECTOR: Now, then, make haste! Where's your ticket?

BANDSMAN (*refreshed*): Aw've lost it!

TICKET COLLECTOR: Nonsense! Feel in your pockets. Ye cannot hev lost it!

BANDSMAN: Aw cannot? Why, man, Aw've lost the *big drum*!

Throughout this volume there runs a series of drawings of cute kiddies above the most distressingly cute captions. If the researcher rapidly tires of the pen-and-ink drawings of the famous George Louis Palmella Busson Du Maurier ("the gentle, graceful satirist of modern fashionable life"), it is perhaps mainly because of the gags he is given to illustrate. I select the ickiest of them. A mother is about to give a dose of medicine to a two-year-old girl:

MASTER GEORGE (*whispers*): I say! Kitty! Has mamma been telling you she'd give you "a lovely spoonful of delicious currant jelly, O so nice, so very nice"?

KITTY: Ess! Cullen' jelly! O so ni', so welly ni'!

MASTER GEORGE: THEN DON'T TAKE IT!

Du Maurier husbands and wives are pictured engaged in what are surely the most depressing conversations ever recorded in the history of civilized man. I quote the first, but not necessarily the worst, of those I come to in my grim notes:

"Well, Dearest, where have you been tonight? 'Monday Pops' again?"

"No, Celia, I have spent a most instructive evening with the 'Anthropological Society'."

"The 'Anthropohowmuch', Darling?"

"The 'Anthropo*logical*', Celia! Are you deaf?"

"How nice! And where do they 'Anthropo*lodge*', Duckums?"

I shall end my discussion of this fond old volume with a caption that, for its simplicity and point, rose out of these fusty yellow pages like a little cool wind. I like to think this is one the author of "Trilby" thought up himself. It appears under a drawing of a dowager in a carriage drawn by two horses and surmounted by a coachman and a footman. The lady has just given alms to a poverty-stricken woman whose ragged children are gathered about her knees:

GRATEFUL RECIPIENT: Bless you, my lady! May we meet in Heaven!

HAUGHTY DONOR: Good Gracious! Drive on, Jarvis!

It grieves me to report that *Punch* was unable to let it go at that. In parentheses and italics there follows this explanatory line: "She had evidently read Dr. Johnson, who 'didn't care to meet certain people *any*where'." Just in case you hadn't caught on.

In the year 1863 (our third and last volume runs from July, '63, to July, '65) the newly married Edward and Alexandra were cheered everywhere they went. The great Blondin was walking the tightrope in the Crystal Palace and a young woman who imitated him at a small-town carnival fell and broke her neck. The Russians were beating up the Poles, and Schleswig-Holstein was the Czecho-Slovakia of the year – and of the next. Louis Napoleon announced that "the improvements brought about by civilization would render war still more destructive." Disraeli said, "The condition of Europe is one of very grave character. Let us be sure, if we go to war, first of all that it is a necessary and just war." The Japanese killed an Englishman named Richardson and "committed a savage assault" on an English woman and two friends. Garibaldi visited London and the three-hundredth anniversary of Shakespeare's birthday was celebrated. *Punch* was irritated by the clamor in the streets caused by organ-grinders and hurdy-gurdy men and hucksters selling watercress and prawns. There is no mention in the volume of what must have been to *Punch* one of the minor events of the early sixties: the battle of Gettysburg.

Mr. Punch's snipes and jibes at Abraham Lincoln and the cause of the North are too well known to call for an extended examination, but the researcher will cite two because he wants to append some notes of his own to them:

Instead of *Habeas Corpus* in the United States, which has been suspended, it is now, in the case of the prisoner who is arbitrarily arrested, ABE who has *corpus*. [Researcher's Note: The English government, which was apparently unswayed by *Punch*, suspended the right of habeas corpus in Ireland in 1866.]

LATEST AMERICAN TELEGRAMS (1864)

Grant reduced to grunt.
Sheridan's Rivals successful
Hunter hunted.
Pillow on Sherman's rear.
[Researcher's Note: The Encyclopedia Americana on Pillow, Gideon J., American soldier: "After 1861 he did not figure in any battle save Murfreesboro, in which he had a courtesy command." Murfreesboro was fought some twenty months before *Punch*'s little crack.]

You might also be interested in a diatribe printed January 21, 1865, and headed "To the Yankee Braggarts":

This American crisis is one which is only to be met by the most unmitigated Swagger, and Mr. Punch, hastily constituting himself Head Swaggerer to the English Nation, hereby answers the Yankee journals "with shouts as loud and shrieks as fierce as their own". [Researcher's Note: Somebody had got off some remarks in America about our being able to lick England.] War with England, indeed, you long-faced, wizened, ugly, ignorant Occidentals! Defy the flag that has braved a thousand years the battle and the breeze? Laugh at the Lion and give umbrage to the Unicorn? Bah! Bosh! Shut up! Tremble!

It goes on to say that one Sir Hugh Rose could go over and lick the whole United States. This happened to be the first time I had ever heard of Sir Hugh, but maybe Grant and Lee knew who he was.

The end to all this is well known: Tenniel drew a touching cartoon showing Britannia laying a wreath on Lincoln's bier and Tom Taylor wrote an equally famous and equally touching poem eating all of *Punch's* nasty words and all of Tenniel's nasty drawings. (This, incidentally, was the year that "Alice in Wonderland" was published, the book that gave Mr. Tenniel something really important to do. I find no mention of it in *Punch*.)

Lincoln and the North might be forgiven, but America's pernicious invention of new words wasn't. "If the pure well of English is to remain undefiled," said Mr. Punch, "no Yankee should be allowed henceforth to throw mud into it. It is a form of verbal expectoration that is most profane, most detestable." He gives you an idea of what he has in mind a few pages farther on. Two American ladies are pictured at a dance, with a young beau standing by. Says one of the ladies (under the heading "Yet Another Americanism"): "Here, Maria, hold my coat while I have a fling with the stranger."

American ladies were invariably represented as pretty and well shaped in spite of Mr. Punch's purple anger at one Nathaniel Hawthorne, sometime American consul at Liverpool, who had brought out a book about England "thoroughly saturated with what seems ill-nature and spite" and making a "savage onslaught upon our women". Excerpts are quoted, but I have space for only one: "English girls seemed to me all homely alike. They seemed to be country lasses, of sturdy and wholesome aspect, with coarse-grained, cabbage-rosy cheeks. . . . How unlike the trim little damsels of my native land!" Mr. Punch hopes that Mr. Hawthorne will go on to write an autobiography, for Mr. Punch is "very partial to essays on the natural history of half-civilized animals".

I will close this survey with a typical illustrated joke of those years of pain and sorrow. It is labelled "Gentle Rebuke" and the caption will give you some idea of what the drawing is like:

OLD GENTLEMAN: How charmingly that young lady sings! Pray, who composed the beautiful song she has just favored us with?

LADY OF THE HOUSE: Oh, it is by Mendelssohn.

OLD GENTLEMAN: Ah! One of his famous "Songs without Words," I suppose.

(Moral – Young ladies, when you sing, pronounce your words carefully, and then you will not expose unmusical old gentlemen to making such ridiculous mistakes as the above.)

Has anybody got any bound copies of old almanacs?

7

THE MAN WHO HATED MOONBAUM

After they had passed through the high, grilled gate they walked for almost a quarter of a mile, or so it seemed to Tallman. It was very dark; the air smelled sweet; now and then leaves brushed against his cheek or forehead. The little, stout man he was following had stopped talking, but Tallman could hear him breathing. They walked on for another minute. "How we doing?" Tallman asked, finally. "Don't ask me questions!" snapped the other man. "Nobody asks me questions! You'll learn." The hell I will, thought Tallman, pushing through the darkness and the fragrance and the mysterious leaves; the hell I will, baby; this is the last time you'll ever see me. The knowledge that he was leaving Hollywood within twenty-four hours gave him a sense of comfort.

There was no longer turf or gravel under his feet; there was something that rang flatly: tile, or flagstones. The little man began to walk more slowly and Tallman almost bumped into him. "Can't we have a light?" said Tallman.

"There you go!" shouted his guide. "Don't get me screaming! What are you trying to do to me?" "I'm not trying to do anything to you," said Tallman. "I'm trying to find out where we're going."

The other man had come to a stop and seemed to be groping around. "First it's wrong uniforms," he said, "then it's red fire – red fire in Scotland, red fire three hundred years ago! I don't know why I ain't crazy!" Tallman could make out the other man dimly, a black, gesturing blob. "You're doing all right," said Tallman. Why did I ever leave the Brown Derby with this guy? he asked himself. Why did I ever let him bring me to his house – if he has a house? Who the hell does he think he is?

Tallman looked at his wristwatch; the dial glowed wanly in the immense darkness. He was a little drunk, but he could see that it was half past three in the morning. "Not trying to do anything to me, he says!" screamed the little man. "Wasn't his fault! It's never anybody's fault! They give me ten thousand dollars' worth of Sam Browne belts for Scotch Highlanders and it's nobody's fault!" Tallman was beginning to get his hangover headache. "I want a light!" he said. "I want a drink! I want to know where the hell I am!" "That's it! Speak out!" said the other. "Say what you think! I like a man who knows where he is. We'll get along." "Contact!" said Tallman. "Camera! Lights! Get out that hundred-year-old brandy you were talking about."

The response to this was a soft flood of rose-colored radiance; the little man had somehow found a light switch in the dark. God knows where, thought Tallman; probably on a tree. They were in a courtyard paved with enormous flagstones which fitted together with mosaic perfection. The light revealed the dark stones of a building which looked like the Place de la Concorde side of the Crillon. "Come on, you people!" said the little man. Tallman looked behind him, half expecting to see the shadowy forms of Scottish Highlanders, but there was nothing but the shadows of trees and of oddly shaped plants closing in on the courtyard. With a key as small as a dime, the little man opened a door that was fifteen feet high and made of wood six inches thick.

Marble stairs tumbled down like Niagara into a grand canyon of a living room. The steps of the two men sounded sharp and clear on the stairs, died in the soft depths of an immensity of carpet in the living room. The ceiling towered above them. There were highlights on dark wood medallions, on burnished shields, on silver curves and edges. On one wall a forty-foot tapestry hung from the ceiling to within a few feet of the floor. Tallman was looking at this when his companion grasped his arm. "The second rose!" he said. "The second rose from the right!" Tallman pulled away. "One of us has got to snap out of this, baby," he said. "How about that brandy?" "Don't interrupt me!" shouted his host. "That's what Whozis whispers to What's-His-Name – greatest love story in the world, if I do say so myself – king's wife mixed up in it – knights riding around with spears – Whozis writes her a message made out of twigs bent together to make words: 'I love you' – sends it floating down a stream past her window – they got her locked in – goddamnedest thing in the history of pictures. Where was I? Oh – 'Second rose from the right,' she says. Why? Because she seen it twitch, she seen it move. What's-His-Name is bending over her, kissing her maybe. He whirls around and shoots an arrow at the rose – second from the right, way up high there – down comes the whole tapestry, weighs eleven hundred pounds, and out rolls this spy, shot through the heart. What's-His-Name sent him to watch the lovers." The little man began to pace up and down the deep carpet. Tallman lighted a fresh cigarette from his glowing stub and sat down in an enormous chair. His host came to a stop in front of the chair and shook his finger at its occupant.

"Look," said the little man. "I don't know who you are and I'm telling you this. You could ruin me, but I got to tell you. I get Moonbaum here – I get Moonbaum himself here – you can ask Manny or Sol – I get the best arrow shot in the world here to fire that arrow for What's-His-Name – "

"Tristram," said Tallman. "Don't prompt me!" bellowed the little man. "For Tristram. What happens? Do I know he's got arrows you shoot bears with? Do I know he ain't got caps on 'em? If I got to know that, why do I have Mitnik? Moonbaum is sitting right there – the tapestry comes down and out rolls this guy, shot through the heart – only the arrow is in his stomach. So what happens? So Moonbaum laughs! That makes Moonbaum laugh! The greatest love story in the history of pictures, and Moonbaum laughs!" The little man raced over to a large chest, opened it, took out a cigar, stuck it in his mouth, and resumed his pacing. "How do you like it?" he shouted. "I love it," said Tallman. "I love every part of it. I always have." The little man raised his hands above his head. "He loves it! He hears one – maybe two – scenes, and he loves every part of it! Even Moonbaum don't know how it comes out, and you love every part of it!" The little man was standing before Tallman's chair again, shaking his cigar at him. "The story got around," said Tallman. "These things leak out. Maybe you talk when you're drinking. What about that brandy?"

The little man walked over and took hold of a bell rope on the wall, next to the tapestry. "Moonbaum laughs like he's dying," he said. "Moonbaum laughs like he's seen Chaplin." He dropped the bell rope. "I hope you really got that hundred-year-old brandy," said Tallman. "Don't keep telling me what you hope!" howled the little man. "Keep listening to what I hope!" He pulled the bell rope savagely. "Now we're getting somewhere," said Tallman. For the first time the little man went to a chair and sat down; he chewed on his unlighted cigar. "Do you know what Moonbaum wants her called?" he demanded, lowering his heavy lids. "I can guess," said Tallman. "Isolde." "Birds of a feather!" shouted his host. "Horses of the same color! Isolde! Name of God, man, you can't call a woman Isolde! What do I want her called?" "You have me there," said Tallman. "I want her called Dawn," said the little man, getting up out of his chair. "It's short, ain't it? It's sweet, ain't it? You can say it, can't you?" "To get back to that brandy," said Tallman, "who is supposed to answer that bell?" "Nobody is supposed to answer it," said the little man. "That don't ring, that's a fake bell rope; it don't ring anywhere. I got it to remind me of an idea Moonbaum ruined. Listen: Louisiana mansion – guy with seven daughters – old-Southern-colonel stuff – Lionel Barrymore could play it – we open on a room that looks like a million dollars – Barrymore crosses and pulls the bell rope. What happens?" "Nothing," said Tallman. "You're crazy!" bellowed the little man. "Part of the wall falls in! Out flies a crow – in walks a goat, maybe – the place has gone to seed, see? It's just a hulk of its former self, it's a shallows!" He turned and walked out of the room. It took him quite a while.

When he came back, he was carrying a bottle of brandy and two huge brandy glasses. He poured a great deal of brandy into each glass and handed one to Tallman. "You and Mitnik!" he said, scornfully. "Pulling walls out of Southern mansions. Crows you give me, goats you give me! What the hell kind of effect is that?" "I could have a bad idea," said Tallman, raising his glass. "Here's to Moonbaum. May he maul things over in his mind all night and never get any spontanuity into 'em." "I drink nothing to Moonbaum," said the little man. "I hate Moonbaum. You know where they catch that crook – that guy has a little finger off one hand and wears a glove to cover it up? What does Moonbaum want? Moonbaum wants the little finger to *flap*! What do I want? I want it stuffed. What do I want it stuffed with? Sand. Why?" "I know," said Tallman. "So that when he closes his hand over the head of his cane, the little finger sticks our stiffly, giving him away." The little man seemed to leap into the air; his brandy splashed out of his glass. "Suitcase!" he screamed. "Not cane! Suitcase! He grabs hold of a suitcase!" Tallman didn't say anything; he closed his eyes and sipped his brandy; it was wonderful brandy. He looked up presently to find his host staring at him with a resigned expression in his eyes. "All right, then, suitcase," the little man said. "Have it suitcase. We won't fight about details. I'm trying to tell you my story. I don't tell my stories to everybody." "Richard Harding Davis stole that finger gag – used it in 'Gallegher'," said Tallman. "You could sue him." The little man walked over to his chair and flopped into it. "He's beneath me," he said. "He's beneath me like the dirt. I ignore him."

Tallman finished his brandy slowly. His host's chin sank upon his chest; his heavy eyelids began to close. Tallman waited several minutes and then tiptoed over to the marble stairs. He took off his shoes and walked up the stairs, carefully. He had the heavy door open when the little man shouted at him. "Birds of a feather, all of you!" he shouted. "You can tell Moonbaum I said so! Shooting guys out of tapestries!" "I'll tell him," said Tallman. "Good night. The brandy was wonderful." The little man was not listening. He was pacing the floor again, gesturing with an empty brandy glass in one hand and the unlighted cigar in the other. Tallman stepped out into the cool air of the courtyard and put on one shoe and laced it. The heavy door swung shut behind him with a terrific crash. He picked up the other shoe and ran wildly toward the trees and the oddly shaped plants. It was daylight now. He could see where he was going.

8

DEATH IN THE ZOO

Naturalists, who are easily baffled by the behaviour of animals, are still wondering why Big Bill, a polar bear at the Fleishhacker Zoo in San Francisco, killed his mate, Min, so unexpectedly. Bill was lying down, strumming at the headboard with his fingers, dreaming of the ice floes or trying to remember where he had put something, when Min tiptoed into the room. "Tiptoeing again," thought Bill, "like a gahdarn poodle dog."

What she said and did in the next few minutes we shall reconstruct later. At the end of it, Bill rolled out of bed and killed her, after which he dragged her thirty feet to a pool of water and held her under for several minutes, to make sure.

I saw the male polar bear at the Central Park Zoo duck his mate one Sunday last April. He grabbed her ear, pulled her head under, kept her there ten seconds or so, and then let her go, growling, half-playfully, "That's for nothing." The Central Park polar bears seem to like each other, which is a break for the zoo attendants, the homicide squad, and the female bear.

Perhaps the principal trouble with American zoos, as regards bears, is that the men in charge of them think that all female bears look alike to a male bear. This conclusion, arrived at from the premise that all female bears look alike to the men in the zoo, is unfortunate to the point of being deadly. To a male polar bear, female polar bears are as different as thumbprints to a G-man. A male polar bear likes only about one female in every fifty he comes across in a day's courting swim. Some bears swim seventy-five miles along a bear-infested coast before they find a female cute enough to bother with.

Not knowing this, the Fleishhacker Zoo men brought Bill a mate one spring that he couldn't abide. She put starch into everything she washed and cheese into everything she cooked; what is more, she kept scratching constantly. Bill swatted her out of existence one day as nonchalantly as if she had been a fly.

He was still grumbling about mating conditions in California when the Fleishhacker people brought him still another mate, rousing him from dreams of the Arctic, where a man can have his pick of a thousand gals. "Lookit, Bill," they said, "the lady of our choice!" Bill noted that she smelled faintly like a Los Angeles roadateria, and that she tacked slightly to the left in lumbering, which was going to be bad since he tacked to the right. Furthermore, she giggled. When the Zoo men left, Bill told the newcomer to stay out of his way, and he went back to the cave and lay down.

When Bill did not come out for several days, Min took to tiptoeing in to see if he wanted a glass of water. She would fiddle with doilies, empty ash trays, wash out his briar pipe with soap and water, open the window if it was shut and shut it if it was open. Once she felt his forehead to see if he had a fever and Bill took a cut at her, but missed. She fled, screaming.

When Bill didn't come out for several more days (he felt fine, but he didn't want to come out), she decided that he was sick, and she determined to take his temperature. She tiptoed in and stuck a thermometer in his mouth before he knew what was happening. Bill watched her tidy up his bureau, putting his socks, handkerchiefs and shirts, which had all been in one drawer, neatly into separate drawers. When she started hanging his ties on a patented nickel-plated cedarwood tie-rack which clasped them in such a way that you couldn't get them off unless you knew how to work the automatic clip-shift tie-release, Bill leaped out of bed and roared into action. He finished off her, the thermometer, and the tie-rack before anybody could stop him. "They turned hoses on me," he said later, "and that helped. I was getting pretty hot."

The Fleishhacker people are probably looking for another mate for Big Bill right now. Well, I have done all *I* can.

9

WHAT DO YOU MEAN IT WAS BRILLIG?

I was sitting at my typewriter one afternoon several weeks ago, staring at a piece of blank white paper, when Della walked in. "They are here with the reeves," she said. It did not surprise me that they were. With a colored woman like Della in the house it would not surprise me if they showed up with the toves. In Della's afternoon it is always brillig; she could outgrabe a mome rath on any wabe in the world. Only Lewis Carroll would have understood Della completely. I try hard enough. "Let them wait a minute," I said. I got out the big Century Dictionary and put it on my lap and looked up "reeve." It is an interesting word, like all of Della's words; I found out that there are four kinds of reeves. "Are they here with strings of onions?" I asked. Della said they were not. "Are they here with enclosures or pens for cattle, poultry, or pigs; sheep-folds?" Della said no sir. "Are they here with administrative officers?" From a little nearer the door Della said no again. "Then they've got to be here," I said, "with some females of the common European sandpiper." These scenes of ours take as much out of Della as they do out of me, but she is not a woman to be put down by a crazy man with a dictionary. "They are here with the reeves for the windas," said Della with brave stubbornness. Then, of course, I understood what they were there with: they were there with the Christmas wreaths for the windows. "Oh, *those* reeves!' I said. We were both greatly relieved; we both laughed. Della and I never quite reach the breaking point; we just come close to it.

Della is a New England colored woman with nothing of the South in her accent; she doesn't say "d" for "th" and she pronounces her "r"s. Hearing her talk in the next room, you might not know at first that she was colored. You might not know till she said some such thing as, "Do you want cretonnes in the soup tonight?" (She makes wonderful cretonnes for the soup.) I have not found out much about Della's words, but I have learned a great deal about her background. She told me one day that she has three brothers and that one of them works into a garage and another works into an incinerator where they burn the refuge. The one that works into the incinerator has been working into it since the Armitage. That's what Della does to you; she gives you incinerator perfectly and then she comes out with the Armitage. I spent most of an hour one afternoon trying to figure out what was wrong with the Armitage; I thought of Armistead and armature and Armentières, and when I finally hit on Armistice it sounded crazy. It still does. Della's third and youngest brother is my favorite; I think he'll be yours, too, and everybody else's. His name is Arthur and it seems that he has just passed, with commendably high grades, his silver-service eliminations. Della is delighted about that, but she is not half so delighted about it as I am.

Della came to our house in Connecticut some months ago, trailing her glory of cloudiness. I can place the date for you approximately: it was while there was still a great many fletchers about. "The lawn is full of fletchers," Della told me one morning, shortly after she arrived, when she brought up my orange juice. "You mean neighbors?" I said. "This early?" By the way she laughed I knew that fletchers weren't people; at least not people of flesh and blood. I got dressed and went downstairs and looked up the word in the indispensable Century. A fletcher, I found, is a man who makes arrows. I decided, but without a great deal of conviction, that there couldn't be any arrow-makers on my lawn at that hour in the morning and at this particular period in history. I walked cautiously out the back door and around to the front of the house – and there they were. I don't know many birds but I do know flickers. A flicker is a bird which, if it were really named fletcher, would be called flicker by all the colored cooks in the United States. Out of a mild curiosity I looked up "flicker" in the dictionary and I discovered that he is a bird of several aliases. When Della brought my toast and coffee into the dining room I told her about this. "Fletchers," I said, "are also golden-winged woodpeckers, yellowhammers, and high-holders." For the first time Della gave me the look that I was to recognize later, during the scene about the reeves. I have become very familiar with that look and I believe I know the thoughts that lie behind it. Della was puzzled at first because I work at home instead of in an office, but I think she has it figured out now. This man, she thinks, used to work into an office like anybody else, but he had to be sent to an institution; he got well enough to come home from the institution, but he is still not well enough to go back to the office. I could have avoided all these suspicions, of course, if I had simply come out in the beginning and corrected Della when she got words wrong. Coming at her obliquely with a dictionary only enriches the confusion; but I wouldn't have it any other way. I share with Della a form of escapism that is the most mystic and satisfying flight from actuality I have ever known. It may not always comfort me, but it never ceases to beguile me.

Every Thursday when I drive Della to Waterbury in the car for her day off, I explore the dark depths and the strange recesses of her nomenclature. I found out that she had been married for ten years but was now divorced; that is, her husband went away one day and never came back. When I asked her what he did for a living, she said he worked into a dove-wedding. "Into a what?" I asked. "Into a dove-wedding," said Della. It is one of the words I haven't figured out yet, but I am still working on it. "Where are you from, Mr. Thurl?" she asked me one day. I told her Ohio, and she said, "Ooooh, to be sure!" as if I had given her a clue to my crazy definitions, my insensitivity to the ordinary household nouns, and my ignorance of the commoner migratory birds. "Semantics, Ohio," I said. "Why, there's one of them in Massachusetts, too," said Della. "The one I mean," I told her, "is bigger and more confusing." "I'll bet it is," said Della.

Della told me the other day that she had had only one sister, a beautiful girl who died when she was twenty-one. "That's too bad," I said. "What was the matter?" Della had what was the matter at her tongue's tip. "She got tuberculosis from her teeth," she said, "and it went all through her symptom." I didn't know what to say to that except that my teeth were all right but that my symptom could probably be easily gone all through. "You work too much with your brain," said Della. I knew she was trying to draw me out about my brain and what had happened to it so that I could no longer work into an office, but I changed the subject. There is no doubt that Della is considerably worried about my mental condition. One morning when I didn't get up till noon because I had been writing letters until three o'clock, Della told my wife at breakfast what was the matter with me. "His mind works so fast his body can't keep up with it," she said. This diagnosis has shaken me not a little. I have decided to sleep longer and work less. I know exactly what will happen to me if my mind gets so far ahead of my body that my body can't catch up with it. They will come with a reeve and this time it won't be a red-and-green one for the window, it will be a black one for the door.

10

INTERVIEW WITH A LEMMING

The weary scientist, tramping through the mountains of northern Europe in the winter weather, dropped his knapsack and prepared to sit on a rock.

"Careful, brother," said a voice.

"Sorry," murmured the scientist, noting with some surprise that a lemming which he had been about to sit on had addressed him. "It is a source of considerable astonishment to me," said the scientist, sitting down beside the lemming, "that you are capable of speech."

"You human beings are always astonished," said the lemming, "when any other animal can do anything you can. Yet there are many things animals can do that you cannot, such as stridulate, or chirr, to name just one. To stridulate, or chirr, one of the minor achievements of the cricket, your species is dependent on the intestines of the sheep and the hair of the horse."

"We are a dependent animal," admitted the scientist.

"You are an amazing animal," said the lemming.

"We have always considered you rather amazing, too," said the scientist. "You are perhaps the most mysterious of creatures."

"If we are going to indulge in adjectives beginning with 'm'," said the lemming, sharply, "let me apply a few to your species – murderous, maladjusted, maleficent, malicious and muffle-headed."

"You find our behaviour as difficult to understand as we do yours?"

"You, as you would say, said it," said the lemming. "You kill, you mangle, you torture, you imprison, you starve each other. You cover the nurturing earth with cement, you cut down elm trees to put up institutions for people driven insane by the cutting down of elm trees, you – "

"You could go on all night like that," said the scientist, "listing our sins and our shames."

"I could go on all night and up to four o'clock tomorrow afternoon," said the lemming. "It just happens that I have made a lifelong study of the self-styled higher animal. Except for one thing, I know all there is to know about you, and a singularly dreary, dolorous and distasteful store of information it is, too, to use only adjectives beginning with 'd'."

"You say you have made a lifelong study of my species – " began the scientist.

"Indeed I have," broke in the lemming. "I know that you are cruel, cunning and carnivorous, sly, sensual and selfish, greedy, gullible and guileful – "

"Pray don't wear yourself out," said the scientist,

quietly. "It may interest you to know that I have made a lifelong study of lemmings, just as you have made a lifelong study of people. Like you, I have found but one thing about my subject which I do not understand."

"And what is that?" asked the lemming.

"I don't understand," said the scientist, "why you lemmings all rush down to the sea and drown yourselves."

"How curious," said the lemming. "The one thing I don't understand is why you human beings don't."

11

YOU COULD LOOK IT UP

It all begun when we dropped down to C'lumbus, Ohio, from Pittsburgh to play a exhibition game on our way out to St. Louis. It was gettin' on into September, and though we'd been leadin' the league by six, seven games most of the season, we was now in first place by a margin you could 'a' got it into the eye of a thimble, bein' only a half a game ahead of St. Louis. Our slump had given the boys the leapin' jumps, and they was like a bunch a old ladies at a lawn fete with a thunderstorm comin' up, runnin' around snarlin' at each other, eatin' bad and sleepin' worse, and battin' for a team average of maybe .186. Half the time nobody'd speak to nobody else, without it was to bawl 'em out.

Squawks Magrew was managin' the boys at the time, and he was darn near crazy. They called him "Squawks" 'cause when things was goin' bad he lost his voice, or perty near lost it, and squealed at you like a little girl you stepped on her doll or somethin'. He yelled at everybody and wouldn't listen to nobody, without maybe it was me. I'd been trainin' the boys for ten year, and he'd take more lip from me than from anybody else. He knowed I was smarter'n him, anyways, like you're goin' to hear.

This was thirty, thirty-one year ago; you could look it up, 'cause it was the same year C'lumbus decided to call itself the Arch City, on account of a lot of iron arches with electric-light bulbs into 'em which stretched acrost High Street. Thomas Albert Edison sent 'em a telegram, and they was speeches and maybe even President Taft opened the celebration by pushin' a button. It was a great week for the Buckeye capital, which was why they got us out there for this exhibition game.

Well, we just lose a double-header to Pittsburgh, 11 to 5 and 7 to 3, so we snarled all the way to C'lumbus, where we put up at the Chittaden Hotel, still snarlin'. Everybody was tetchy, and when Billy Klinger took a sock at Whitey Cott at breakfast, Whitey threw marmalade all over his face.

"Blind each other, whatta I care?" says Magrew. "You can't see nothin' anyways."

C'lumbus win the exhibition game, 3 to 2, whilst Magrew set in the dugout, mutterin' and cursin' like a fourteen-year-old Scotty. He bad-mouthed everybody on the ball club and he bad-mouthed everybody offa the ball club, includin' the Wright brothers, who, he claimed, had yet to build a airship big enough for any of our boys to hit it with a ball bat.

"I wisht I was dead," he says to me. "I wisht I was in heaven with the angels."

I told him to pull hisself together, 'cause he was drivin' the boys crazy, the way he was goin' on, sulkin' and bad-mouthin' and whinin'. I was older'n he was and smarter'n he was, and he knowed it. I was ten times smarter'n he was about this Pearl du Monville, first time I ever laid eyes on the little guy, which was one of the saddest days of my life.

Now, most people name of Pearl is girls, but this Pearl du Monville was a man, if you could call a fella a man who was only thirty-four, thirty-five inches high. Pearl du Monville was a midget. He was part French and part Hungarian, and maybe even part Bulgarian or somethin'. I can see him now, a sneer on his little pushed-in pan, swingin' a bamboo cane and smokin' a big cigar. He had a gray suit with a big black check into it, and he had a gray felt hat with one of them rainbow-colored hatbands onto it, like the young fellas wore in them days. He talked like he was talkin' into a tin can, but he didn't have no foreign accent. He might a been fifteen or he might a been a hundred, you couldn't tell. Pearl du Monville.

After the game with C'lumbus, Magrew headed straight for the Chittaden bar – the train for St. Louis wasn't goin' for three, four hours – and there he set, drinkin' rye and talkin' to this bartender.

"How I pity me, brother," Magrew was tellin' this bartender. "How I pity me." That was alwuz his favorite tune. So he was settin' there, tellin' this bartender how heartbreakin' it was to be manager of a bunch a blind-folded circus clowns, when up pops this Pearl du Monville outa nowheres.

It gave Magrew the leapin' jumps. He thought at first

maybe the D.T.'s had come back on him; he claimed he'd had 'em once, and little guys had popped up all around him, wearin' red, white and blue hats.

"Go on, now!" Magrew yells. "Get away from me!"

But the midget clumb up on a chair acrost the table from Magrew and says, "I seen that game today, Junior, and you ain't got no ball club. What you got there, Junior," he says, "is a side show."

"Whatta ya mean, 'Junior'?" says Magrew, touchin' the little guy to satisfy hisself he was real.

"Don't pay him no attention, mister," says the bartender. "Pearl calls everybody 'Junior', 'cause it alwuz turns out he's a year older'n anybody else."

"Yeh?" says Magrew. "How old is he?"

"How old are you, Junior?" says the midget.

"Who, me? I'm fifty-three," says Magrew.

"Well, I'm fifty-four," says the midget.

Magrew grins and asts him what he'll have, and that was the beginnin' of their beautiful friendship, if you don't care what you say.

Pearl du Monville stood up on his chair and waved his cane around and pretended like he was ballyhooin' for a circus. "Right this way, folks!" he yells. "Come on in and see the greatest collection of freaks in the world! See the armless pitchers, see the eyeless batters, see the infielders with five thumbs!" and on and on like that, feedin' Magrew gall and handin' him a laugh at the same time, you might say.

You could hear him and Pearl du Monville hootin' and hollerin' and singin' way up to the fourth floor of the

81

Chittaden, where the boys was packin' up. When it come time to go the station, you can imagine how disgusted we was when we crowded into the doorway of that bar and seen them two singin' and goin' on.

"Well, well, well," says Magrew, lookin' up and spottin' us. "Look who's here. . . . Clowns, this is Pearl du Monville, a monseer of the old, old school. . . . Don't shake hands with 'em Pearl, 'cause their fingers is made of chalk and would bust right off in your paws," he says, and he starts guffawin' and Pearl starts titterin' and we stand there givin' 'em the iron eye, it bein' the lowest ebb a ballclub manager'd got hisself down to since the national pastime was started.

Then the midget begun givin' us the ballyhoo. "Come on in!" he says, wavin' his cane. "See the legless base runners, see the outfielders with the butter fingers, see the southpaw with the arm of a little chee-ild!"

Then him and Magrew begun to hoop and holler and nudge each other till you'd of thought this little guy was the funniest guy than even Charlie Chaplin. The fellas filed outa the bar without a word and went on up to the Union Depot, leavin' me to handle Magrew and his newfound crony.

Well, I got 'em outa there finely. I had to take the little guy along, 'cause Magrew had a holt onto him like a vise and I couldn't pry him loose.

"He's comin' along as masket," says Magrew, holdin' the midget in the crouch of his arm like a football. And come along he did, hollerin' and protestin' and beatin' at Magrew with his little fists.

"Cut it out, will ya, Junior?" the little guy kept whinin'. "Come on, leave a man loose, will ya, Junior?"

But Junior kept a holt onto him and begun yellin', "See the guys with the glass arm, see the guys with the cast-iron brains, see the fielders with the feet on their wrists!"

So it goes, right through the whole Union Depot, with people starin' and catcallin', and he don't put the midget down till he get him through the gates.

"How'm I goin' to go along without no toothbrush?" the midget asts. "What'm I goin' to do without no other suit?" he says.

"Doc here," says Magrew, meanin' me – "doc here will look after you like you was his own son, won't you, doc?"

I give him the iron eye, and he finely got on the train and prob'ly went to sleep with his clothes on.

This left me alone with the midget. "Lookit," I says to him. "Why don't you go on home now? Come mornin', Magrew'll forget all about you. He'll prob'ly think you was somethin' he seen in a nightmare maybe. And he ain't goin' to laugh so easy in the mornin', neither," I says. "So why don't you go on home?"

"Nix," he says to me. "Skiddoo," he says, "Twenty-three for you," and he tosses his cane up into the vestibule of the coach and clam'ers on up after it like a cat. So that's the way Pearl du Monville come to go to St. Louis with the ball club.

I seen 'em first at breakfast the next day, settin' opposite each other; the midget playin' "Turkey in the Straw" on a harmonium and Magrew starin' at his eggs and bacon like they was a uncooked bird with its feathers still on.

"Remember where you found this?" I says, jerkin' my thumb at the midget. "Or maybe you think they come with breakfast on these trains," I says, bein' a good hand at turnin' a sharp remark in them days.

The midget puts down the harmonium and turns on me. "Sneeze," he says; "your brains is dusty." Then he snaps a couple drops of water at me from a tumbler. "Drown," he says, tryin' to make his voice deep.

Now, both them cracks is Civil War cracks, but you'd of thought they was brand new and the funniest than any crack Magrew'd ever heard in his whole life. He started hoopin' and hollerin', and the midget started hoopin' and hollerin', so I walked on away and set down with Bugs Courtney and Hank Metters, payin' no attention to this weak-minded Damon and Phidias acrost the aisle.

Well, sir, the first game with St. Louis was rained out, and there we was facin' a double-header next day. Like maybe I told you, we lose the last three double-headers we play, makin' maybe twenty-five errors in the six games, which is all right for the intimates of a school for the blind, but is disgraceful for the world's champions. It was too wet to go to the zoo, and Magrew wouldn't let us go to the movies, 'cause they flickered so bad in them days. So we just set around, stewin' and frettin'.

One of the newspaper boys come over to take a pitture of Billy Klinger and Whitey Cott shakin' hands – this reporter'd heard about the fight – and whilst they was standin' there, toe to toe, shakin' hands, Billy give a back lunge and a jerk, and throwed Whitey over his shoulder into a corner of the room, like a sack a salt. Whitey come back at him with a chair, and Bethlehem broke loose in that there room. The camera was tromped to pieces like a berry basket. When we finely got 'em pulled apart, I heard a laugh, and there was Magrew and the midget standin' in the door and givin' us the iron eye.

"Wrasslers," says Magrew, cold-like, "that's what I got for a ball club, Mr. Du Monville, wrasslers – and not very good wrasslers at that, you ast me."

"A man can't be good at everythin'," says Pearl, "but he oughta be good at somethin'."

This sets Magrew guffawin' again, and away they go, the midget taggin' along by his side like a hound dog and handin' him a fast line of so-called comic cracks.

When we went out to face that battlin' St. Louis club in a double-header the next afternoon, the boys was jumpy as tin toys with keys in their back. We lose the first game, 7 to 2, and are trailin', 4 to 0, when the second game ain't but ten minutes old. Magrew set there like a stone statue, speakin' to nobody. Then, in their half a the fourth, somebody singled to center and knocked in two more runs for St. Louis.

That made Magrew squawk. "I wisht one thing," he says. "I wisht I was manager of a old ladies' sewin' circus 'stead of a ball club."

"You are, Junior, you are," says a familyer and disagreeable voice.

It was that Pearl du Monville again, poppin' up outa nowheres, swingin' his bamboo cane and smokin' a cigar that's three sizes too big for his face. By this time we'd finely got the other side out, and Hank Metters slithered a bat acrost the ground, and the midget had to jump to keep both his ankles from bein' broke.

I thought Magrew'd bust a blood vessel. "You hurt Pearl and I'll break your neck!" he yelled.

Hank muttered somethin' and went on up to the plate and struck out.

We managed to get a couple runs acrost in our half a the sixth, but they come back with three more in their half a the seventh, and this was too much for Magrew.

"Come on, Pearl," he says. "we're gettin outa here."

"Where you think you're goin'?" I ast him.

"To the lawyer's again," he says cryptly.

"I didn't know you'd been to the lawyer's once, yet," I says.

"Which that goes to show how much you don't know," he says.

With that, they was gone, and I didn't see 'em the rest of the day, nor know what they was up to, which was a God's blessin'. We lose the nightcap, 9 to 3, and that puts us into second place plenty, and as low in our mind as a ball club can get.

The next day was a horrible day, like anybody that lived through it can tell you. Practice was just over and the St. Louis club was takin' the field, when I hears this strange sound from the stands. It sounds like the nervous whick-erin' a horse gives when he smells somethin' funny on the wind. It was the fans ketchin' sight of Pearl du Monville, like you have prob'ly guessed. The midget had popped up onto the field all dressed up in a minacher club uniform, sox, cap, little letters sewed onto his chest, and all. He was swingin' a kid's bat and the only thing kept him from lookin' like a real ballplayer seen through the wrong end of a microscope was this cigar he was smokin'.

Bugs Courtney reached over and jerked it outa his mouth and throwed it away. "You're wearin' that suit on the playin' field," he says to him, severe as a judge. "You go insultin' it and I'll take you out to the zoo and feed you to the bears."

Pearl just blowed some smoke at him which he still has in his mouth.

Whilst Whitey was foulin' off four or five prior to strikin' out, I went on over to Magrew. "If I was as comic as you," I says, "I'd laugh myself to death," I says. "Is that any way to treat the uniform, makin' a mockery out of it?"

"It might surprise you to know I ain't makin' no mockery outa the uniform," says Magrew. "Pearl du Monville here has been made a bone-of-fida member of this so-called ball club. I fixed it up with the front office by long-distance phone."

"Yeh?" I says. "I can just hear Mr. Dillworth or Bart Jenkins agreein' to hire a midget for the ball club. I can just hear 'em." Mr. Dillworth was the owner of the club and Bart Jenkins was the secretary, and they never stood for no monkey business. "May I be so bold as to inquire," I says, "just what you told 'em?"

"I told 'em," he says, "I wanted to sign up a guy they ain't no pitcher in the league can strike him out."

"Uh-huh," I says, "and did you tell 'em what size of a man he is?"

"Never mind about that," he says. "I got papers on me, made out legal and proper, constitutin' one Pearl du Monville a bone-of-fida member of this former ball club. Maybe that'll shame them big babies into gettin' in there and swingin', knowin' I can replace any one of 'em with a midget, if I have a mind to. A St. Louis lawyer I seen twice tells me it's all legal and proper."

"A St. Louis lawyer would," I says, "seein' nothin' could make him happier than havin' you makin' a mockery outa this one-time baseball outfit," I says.

Well, sir, it'll all be there in the papers of thirty, thirty-one year ago, and you could look it up. The game went along without no scorin' for seven innings, and since they ain't nothin' much to watch but guys poppin' up or strikin' out, the fans pay most of their attention to the goin's-on of Pearl du Monville. He's out there in front a the dugout, turnin' handsprings, balancin' his bat on his chin, walkin' a imaginary line, and so on. The fans clapped and laughed at him, and he ate it up.

So it went up to the last a the eighth, nothin' to nothin', not more'n seven, eight hits all told, and no errors on neither side. Our pitcher gets the first two men out easy in the eighth. Then up come a fella name of Porter or Billings, or some such name, and he lammed one up against the tobacco sign for three bases. The next guy up slapped the first ball out into left for a base hit, and in come the fella from third for the only run of the ball game so far. The crowd yelled, the look a death come onto Magrew's face again, and even the midget quit his tom-foolin'. Their next man fouled out back a third, and we come up for our last bats like a bunch a schoolgirls steppin' into a pool of cold water. I was lower in my mind than I'd been since the day in Nineteen-four when Chesbro throwed the wild pitch in the ninth inning with a man on third and lost the pennant for the Highlanders. I knowed something just as bad was goin' to happen, which shows I'm a clairvoyun, or was then.

When Gordy Mills hit out to second, I just closed my eyes. I opened 'em up again to see Dutch Muller standin' on second, dustin' off his pants, him havin' got his first hit in maybe twenty times to the plate. Next up was Harry Loesing, battin' for our pitcher, and he got a base on balls, walkin' on a fourth one you could a combed your hair with.

Then up come Whitey Cott, our lead-off man. He crotches down in what was prob'ly the most fearsome stanch in organized ball, but all he can do is pop out to short. That brung up Billy Klinger, with two down and a man on first and second. Billy took a cut at one you could a knocked a plug hat offa this here Carnera with it, but then he gets sense enough to wait 'em out, and finely he walks, too, fillin' the bases.

Yes, sir, there you are; the tyin' run on third and the winnin' run on second, first at the ninth, two men down, and Hank Metters comin' to the bat. Hank was built like a Pope-Hartford and he couldn't run no faster'n President Taft, but he had five home runs to his credit for the season, and that wasn't bad in them days. Hank was still hittin' better'n anybody else on the ball club, and it was mighty heartenin', seein' him stridin' up towards the plate. But he never got there.

"Wait a minute!" yells Magrew, jumpin' to his feet. "I'm sendin' in a pinch hitter!" he yells.

You could a heard a bomb drop. When a ballclub manager says he's sendin' in a pinch hitter for the best batter on the club, you know and I know and everybody knows he's lost his holt.

"They're goin' to be sendin' the funny wagon for you, if you don't watch out," I says, grabbin' a holt of his arm.

But he pulled away and run out towards the plate, yellin', "Du Monville battin' for Metters!"

All the fellas begun squawlin' at once, except Hank, and he just stood there starin' at Magrew like he'd gone crazy and was claimin' to be Ty Cobb's grandma or somethin'. Their pitcher stood out there with his hands on his hips and a disagreeable look on his face, and the plate umpire told Magrew to go on and get a batter up. Magrew told him again Du Monville was battin' for Metters, and the St. Louis manager finely got the idea. It brung him outa his dugout, howlin' and bawlin' like he'd lost a female dog and her seven pups.

Magrew pushed the midget towards the plate and he says to him, he says, "Just stand up there and hold that bat on your shoulder. They ain't a man in the world can throw three strikes in there 'fore he throws four balls!" he says.

"I get it, Junior!" says the midget. "He'll walk me and force in the tyin' run!" And he starts on up to the plate as cocky as if he was Willie Keeler.

I don't need to tell you Bethlehem broke loose on that there ball field. The fans got onto their hind legs, yellin' and whistlin', and everybody on the field begun wavin' their arms and hollerin' and shovin'. The plate umpire stalked over to Magrew like a traffic cop, waggin' his jaw and pointin' his finger, and the St. Louis manager kept yellin' like his house was on fire. When Pearl got up to the plate and stood there, the pitcher slammed his glove down onto the ground and started stompin' on it, and they ain't nobody can blame him. He's just walked two normal-sized human bein's, and now here's a guy up to the plate they ain't more'n twenty inches between his knees and his shoulders.

The plate umpire called in the field umpire, and they talked a while, like a couple doctors seein' the bucolic plague or somethin' for the first time. Then the plate umpire come over to Magrew with his arms folded acrost his chest, and he told him to go on and get a batter up, or he'd forfeit the game to St. Louis. He pulled out his watch, but somebody batted it outa his hand in the scufflin', and I thought there'd be a free-for-all, with everybody yellin' and shovin' except Pearl du Monville, who stood up at the plate with his little bat on his shoulder, not movin' a muscle.

Then Magrew played his ace. I seen him pull some papers outa his pocket and show 'em to the plate umpire. The umpire begun lookin' at 'em like they was bills for somethin' he not only never bought it, he never even heard of it. The other umpire studied 'em like they was a death warren, and all this time the St. Louis manager and the fans and the players is yellin' and hollerin'.

Well, sir, they fought about him bein' a midget, and

they fought about him usin' a kid's bat, and they fought about where'd he been all season. They was eight or nine rule books brung out and everybody was thumbin' through 'em, tryin' to find out what it says about midgets, but it don't say nothin' about midgets, 'cause this was somethin' never'd come up in the history of the game before, and nobody'd ever dreamed about it, even when they has nightmares. Maybe you can't send no midgets in to bat nowadays, 'cause the old game's changed a lot, mostly for the worst, but you could then, it turned out.

The plate umpire finely decided the contrack papers was all legal and proper, like Magrew said, so he waved the St. Louis players back to their places and he pointed his finger at their manager and told him to quit hollerin' and get on back in the dugout. The manager says the game is percedin' under protest, and the umpire bawls, "Play ball!" over 'n' above the yellin' and booin', him havin' a voice like a hog-caller.

The St. Louis pitcher picked up his glove and beat at it with his fist six or eight times, and then got set on the mound and studied the situation. The fans realized he was really goin' to pitch to the midget, and they went crazy, hoopin' and hollerin' louder'n ever, and throwin' pop bottles and hats and cushions down onto the field. It took five, ten minutes to get the fans quieted down again, whilst our fellas that was on base set down on the bags and waited. And Pearl du Monville kept standin' up there with the bat on his shoulder, like he'd been told to.

So the pitcher starts studyin' the set-up again, and you got to admit it was the strangest set-up in a ball game since the players cut off their beards and begun wearin' gloves. I wisht I could call the pitcher's name – it wasn't old Barney Pelty nor Nig Jack Powell nor Harry Howell. He was a big right-hander, but I can't call his name. You could look it up. Even in a crotchin' position, the ketcher towers over the midget like the Washington Monument.

The plate umpire tries standin' on his tiptoes, then he tries crotchin' down, and he finely gets hisself into a stance nobody'd ever seen on a ball field before, kinda squattin' down on his hanches.

Well, the pitcher is sore as a old buggy horse in fly time. He slams in the first pitch, hard and wild, and maybe two foot higher'n the midget's head.

"Ball one!" hollers the umpire over 'n' above the racket, 'cause everybody is yellin' worsten ever.

The ketcher goes on out towards the mound and talks to the pitcher and hands him the ball. This time the big right-hander tried a undershoot, and it comes in a little closer, maybe no higher'n a foot, foot and a half above Pearl's head. It would a been a strike with a human bein' in there, but the umpire's got to call it, and he does.

"Ball two!" he bellers.

The ketcher walks on out to the mound again, and the whole infield comes over and gives advice to the pitcher about what they'd do in a case like this, with two balls and no strikes on a batter that oughta be in a bottle of alcohol 'stead of up there at the plate in a big-league game between the teams that is fightin' for first place.

For the third pitch, the pitcher stands there flat-footed and tosses up the ball like he's playin' ketch with a little girl.

Pearl stands there motionless as a hitchin' post, and the ball comes in big and slow and high – high for Pearl, that is, it bein' about on a level with his eyes, or a little higher'n a grown man's knees.

They ain't nothin' else for the umpire to do, so he calls, "Ball three!"

Everybody is onto their feet, hoopin' and hollerin', as the pitcher sets to throw ball four. The St. Louis manager is makin' signs and faces like he was a contorturer, and the infield is givin' the pitcher some more advice about what to do this time. Our boys who was on base stick right onto the bag, runnin' no risk of bein' nipped for the last out.

Well, the pitcher decides to give him a toss again, seein' he come closer with that than with a fast ball. They ain't nobody ever seen a slower ball throwed. It come in big as a balloon and slower'n any ball ever throwed before in the major leagues. It come right in over the plate in front of Pearl's chest, lookin' prob'ly big as a full moon to Pearl. They ain't never been a minute like the minute that followed since the United States was founded by the Pilgrim grandfathers.

Pearl du Monville took a cut at that ball, and he hit it! Magrew give a groan like a pole-axed steer as the ball rolls out in front a the plate into fair territory.

"Fair ball!" yells the umpire, and the midget starts runnin' for first, still carryin' that little bat, and makin' maybe ninety foot an hour. Bethlehem breaks loose on that ball field and in them stands. They ain't never been nothin' like it since creation was begun.

The ball's rollin' slow, on down towards third, goin' maybe eight, ten foot. The infield comes in fast and our boys break from their bases like hares in a brush fire. Everybody is standin' up, yellin' and hollerin', and Magrew is tearin' his hair outa his head, and the midget is scamperin' for first with all the speed of one of them little dashhounds carryin' a satchel in his mouth.

The ketcher gets to the ball first, but he boots it on out past the pitcher's box, the pitcher fallin' on his face tryin' to stop it, the shortstop sprawlin' after it full length and zaggin' it on over towards the second baseman, whilst Muller is scorin' with the tyin' run and Loesing is roundin' third with the winnin' run. Ty Cobb could a made a three-bagger outa that bunt, with everybody fallin' over theirself tryin' to pick the ball up. But Pearl is still maybe fifteen, twenty feet from the bag, toddlin' like a baby and yeepin' like a trapped rabbit, when the second baseman finely gets a holt of that ball and slams it over to first. The first baseman ketches it and stomps on the bag, the base umpire waves Pearl out, and there goes your old ball game, the craziest ball game ever played in the history of the organized world.

Their players start runnin' in, and then I see Magrew. He starts after Pearl, runnin' faster'n any man ever run before. Pearl sees him comin' and runs behind the base umpire's legs and gets a holt onto 'em. Magrew comes up, pantin' and roarin', and him and the midget plays ring-around-a-rosy with the umpire, who keeps shovin' at Magrew with one hand and tryin' to slap the midget loose from his legs with the other.

Finely Magrew ketches the midget, who is still yeepin' like a stuck sheep. He gets holt of that little guy by both his ankles and starts whirlin' him round and round his head like Magrew was a hammer thrower and Pearl was the hammer. Nobody can stop him without gettin' their head knocked off, so everybody just stands there and yells. Then Magrew lets the midget fly. He flies on out towards second, high and fast, like a human home run, headed for the soap sign in center field.

Their shortstop tries to get to him, but he can't make it, and I knowed the little fella was goin' to bust to pieces like a dollar watch on a asphalt street when he hit the ground. But it so happens their center fielder is just crossin' second, and he starts runnin' back, tryin' to get under the midget, who had took to spiralin' like a football 'stead of turnin' head over foot, which give him more speed and more distance.

I know you never seen a midget ketched, and you prob'ly never even seen one throwed. To ketch a midget that's been throwed by a heavy-muscled man and is flyin' through the air, you got to run under him and with him and pull your hands and arms back and down when you ketch him, to break the compact of his body, or you'll bust him in two like a matchstick. I see Bill Lange and Willie Keeler and Tris Speaker make some wonderful ketches in my day, but I never seen nothin' like that center fielder. He goes back and back and still further back and he pulls that midget down outa the air like he was liftin' a sleepin' baby from a cradle. They wasn't a bruise onto him, only his face was the color of cat's meat and he ain't got no air in his chest. In his excitement, the base umpire, who was runnin' back with the center fielder when he ketched Pearl, yells, "Out!" and that give hysteries to the Bethlehem which was ragin' like Niagry on the ball field.

Everybody was hoopin' and hollerin' and yellin' and runnin', with the fans swarmin' onto the field, and the cops tryin' to keep order, and some guys laughin' and some of the women fans cryin', and six or eight of us holdin' onto Magrew to keep him from gettin' at that midget and finishin' him off. Some of the fans picks up the St. Louis pitcher and the center fielder, and starts carryin' 'em around on their shoulders, and they was the craziest goin's-on knowed to the history of organized ball on this side of the 'Lantic Ocean.

I seen Pearl du Monville strugglin' in the arms of a lady fan with a ample bosom, who was laughin' and cryin' at the same time, and him beatin' at her with his little fists and bawlin' and yellin'. He clawed his way loose finely and disappeared in the forest of legs which made that ball field look like it was Coney Island on a hot summer's day.

That was the last I ever seen of Pearl du Monville. I never seen hide nor hair of him from that day to this, and neither did nobody else. He just vanished into the thin of the air, as the fella says. He was ketched for the final out of the ball game and that was the end of him, just like it was the end of the ball game, you might say, and also the end of our losin' streak, like I'm goin' to tell you.

That night we piled onto a train for Chicago, but we wasn't snarlin' and snappin' any more. No, sir, the ice was finely broke and a new spirit come into that ball club. The old zip come back with the disappearance of Pearl du Monville out back a second base. We got to laughin' and talkin' and kiddin' together, and 'fore long Magrew was laughin' with us. He got a human look onto his pan again, and he quit whinin' and complainin' and wishtin' he was in heaven with the angels.

Well, sir, we wiped up that Chicago series, winnin' all four games, and makin' seventeen hits in one of 'em. Funny thing was, St. Louis was so shook up by that last game with us, they never did hit their stride again. Their center fielder took to misjudgin' everything that come his way, and the rest a the fellas followed suit, the way a club'll do when one guy blows up.

'Fore we left Chicago, I and some of the fellas went out and bought a pair of them little baby shoes, which we had 'em golded over and give 'em to Magrew for a souvenir, and he took it all in good spirit. Whitey Cott and Billy Klinger made up and was fast friends again, and we hit our home lot like a ton of dynamite and they was nothin' could stop us from then on.

I don't recollect things as clear as I did thirty, forty year ago. I can't read no fine print no more, and the only person I got to check with on the golden days of the national pastime, as the fella says, is my friend, old Milt Kline, over in Springfield, and his mind ain't as strong as it once was.

He gets Rube Waddell mixed up with Rube Marquard, for one thing, and anybody does that oughta be put away where he won't bother nobody. So I can't tell you the exact margin we win the pennant by. Maybe it was two and a half games, or maybe it was three and a half. But it'll all be there in the newspapers and record books of thirty, thirty-one year ago and, like I was sayin', you could look it up.

12

FOOTNOTE ON THE FUTURE

The scientists, in spite of everything, have begun to look optimistically into the future of Man and of the Universe. Just when I had been led to believe that the human being and his planet had no more hope of a prolonged and improved existence than a lace valentine in hell, word is brought to me by my pageboys that neither the sun nor the mind of man is, after all, going out. Unlimited supplies of hydrogen atoms have been discovered in the sun and billions of unused brain cells have been detected in the cortex of Man. The scientists, who look beyond the little menaces of the mundane moment, are, quite naturally, cheerful.

I remember when the scientists were not so cheerful; I remember when Man and his flimsy globe were doomed. I had become, before the good news arrived, a timid eschatologist, quietly waiting for the finish of this fragile Luna moth we call mortality. In 1910, when I was a stripling of sixteen going on seventeen, the bearded watchers of the skies (at least those in the Middle West) fondly predicted that Halley's Comet was going to strike the planet a staggering blow somewhere between Boise and Boston, knocking it far out into the oblivious Darkness, the incomprehensible Cold. Nothing happened, except that I was left with a curious twitching of my left ear after sundown and a tendency to break into a dog-trot at the striking of a match or the flashing of a lantern.

In the decade that followed the destruction of the world by Mr. Halley's recurrent monument, there were various cosmic alarms and flourishes, mainly dealing with the odds-on probability that the sunspots, which were spreading as rapidly as ulcerative gingivitis, would before long turn the sun into a monstrous black cinder which for several million years would give off a faint buzzing sound, but no heat at all. In the immeasurable sphere of this cold, colossal buzzing no leaf would stir, no voice would cry; there would be no ear to listen. (It was at this period that I began to compose what an old city editor for whom I worked called "morbid pomes".)

In 1933, I think it was – anyway, it was after my best years had been spent, so I didn't worry so much – the universe was reported to be shrinking at an appalling rate and we were given only a few paltry aeons to prepare our species for the end, a handful of millenniums before the indescribable boundaries should close in on us, smothering, without malice or favor, gold-star mothers, collectors of internal revenue, and little laughing girls on their way to school. Since 1933, as everyone knows, we have been imperilled by widely assorted threats of extinction, mainly the even-money chance that the topsoil of the world, in one vast, restless conspiracy of movement, would bury us all, like Leptis Magna, under its soft and whispering oblivion.

The menaces to God's wonderful clockwork have all passed, like the Great Noise over Brooklyn. The universal goose now hangs high. After long and painstaking research, Professor Hans Bethe of Cornell has come out with the announcement that the sun has enough hydrogen atoms to last it twelve thousand million years. There is cheerful news, too, from other cosmic fronts. The topsoil of the earth seems to have settled down – or at least to be biding its time; the universe has quit shrinking and may, indeed, even be expanding, although I don't think so; and a Kansas scientist reports that when Halley's Comet gets back, in 1985, it will be so frayed and fuzzy that it won't be able to cause any really serious trouble. (I will be ninety when Halley's Comet gets back and will no longer much care what happens. I may even be disappointed, in my querulous nonagenarian way, if the famous visitor does not deal California a glancing backhand blow before it goes careening off again into the illimitable spaces upon its unfathomable rounds.)

Now that Man, in spite of his sins, stands a fair chance of lasting another twelve thousand million years, other things being equal, it might be interesting to speculate on what he is going to be like at the end of that time, or even in one twelve-thousandth of that time. There is always, of course, the chance, sun or no sun, that the insects may get him within the next two or three hundred years, but after worrying about this since 1907, I have come to the conclusion that Man will finally master the tiny creatures, in spite of their greater agility and superior cleverness. My confidence in Man's ultimate supremacy over the weevil and the slug has been greatly strengthened by the findings of the late Dr. Frederick Tilney, the eminent brain specialist. After many years of research, Dr. Tilney came to the conclusion that Man is using only one-fourth of his stock of fourteen billion brain cells. In short, he is using only 3,500,000,000 brain cells. Offhand, to the layman, to you and me, this might seem like a great many brain cells to be using, since it runs into ten figures and we Americans are impressed by anything that runs into more than four. We must, however, fight against the kind of complacency which would lead us to sit back and be satisfied with the use of only three and a half billion brain cells. When we wake up in the morning we should not say to ourselves, gleefully, "I am using more than three billion brain cells. Good Lord, think of it!" We should, on the contrary, say, "I am using only one-fourth of the brain cells with which a generous Providence has provided me. Is that any way to live, for God's sake?"

It was Dr. Tilney's belief that when Man begins to use all his brain cells – in a thousand years, say, or ten million – he will become wise enough to put an end to wars, depressions, recessions, and allied evils. Dr. Tilney seemed to believe that a man four times as mentally powerful as we are today would, if handed a rifle by some throwback major who was still using only 3,500,000,000 brain cells, exclaim, "Don't be a fourth-wit, my man," and refuse to go to war. I am sorry that I cannot go the whole way with Dr. Tilney in his sanguine prophecies. What, I keep saying to myself, is to keep Man from becoming four times as ornery, four times as sly and crafty, four times as full of devilishly ingenious devices for the extinction of his species? In the history of mankind the increase of no kind of power has, so far as I can find out, ever moved naturally and inevitably in the direction of the benign. It has, as a matter of fact, almost always tended in the direction of the malignant; don't ask me why, it just has. This tendency, it seems to me, would be especially true of the power of the mind, since it is that very power which is behind all the devilry Man is now up to and always has been up to.

Let us turn our attention for a moment to those prehistoric Americans, Sandia man, Folsom man, and the Minnesota Maid, whose fossilized remains have been dug up from the substrata of this ancient continent. I have no way of knowing for sure, but I venture to say that the cells which were actually functioning in the brains of Sandia, Folsom, and the Maid did not number more than 875,000,000, or about one-fourth as many as are working today in your brain or mine or Mussolini's. Now, it should follow, if Dr. Tilney was on sound ground, that the man of today is four times as pacific and four times as economically sound as Sandia and Folsom. Anybody who has more than eleven hundred cells working in his cortex knows that this is not true. Man, as pacifist and economist, has gone steadily from bad to worse with the development of his brain power through the ages. I view with alarm, therefore, any future increase of his cortical activity.

Let us proceed to another dolorous conclusion. *Time*, the weekly scientific journal, reported some time ago that the Minnesota Maid "apparently fell or was thrown into a Glacial Period lake". How *Time*, always infallible, knew that the Maid either fell or was thrown into the lake I don't know. I should have thought there was also the possibility that, driven to distraction by people who were using only 875,000,000 brain cells, she may have swum quietly out into the lake to drown, of her own accord. However, let us assume that she was thrown. Now, you would think, if Dr. Tilney was right, that the increase of Man's functioning brain cells in the millions of years which have elapsed since the Maid's death would have prompted Man to refrain from throwing Woman into lakes. This is, unhappily, not the case. I estimate, after sitting for half an hour thinking, that more than four times as many women are thrown into lakes in America nowadays as were thrown into them during the era in which the Minnesota Maid lived. How many, at this rate of increase, will be thrown into American lakes twelve thousand million years from now, I leave to your imagination.

The only note of cheer I can strike, in conclusion, is to point out the possibility that, in spite of Dr. Tilney's beliefs, Man may never be able to use more than one-fourth of his brain cells. In that case he is not likely to become much more troublesome than he is now. He is certain, at any rate, not to become four times as troublesome. This is, I know, not much in the way of hope for the future, but it is, after all, something. At any rate, it is all I have to offer.

You may all file out quietly now, with the exception of Miss Winthrop, whom I should like to see for a few moments after class. Miss Winthrop may not be aware of it, but the little song she has chosen to compose especially for this occasion has not been lost upon my ears. I refer, Miss Winthrop, to "The Japanese Sandia Man", which you have been singing quite audibly during the last half-hour of my lecture. The rest of you may go.

13

THE GENTLEMAN IN 916

One of my remarkable collection of colored maids wrote me a letter the other day. This girl, named Maisie, is the one who caused my hair to whiten over night a few years ago by telling me when I got home one gloomy November evening, tired and jumpy, that there was something wrong with the doom-shaped thing in the kitchen. This monstrous menace turned out, too late to save my reason, to be the dome- (to her) shaped thing on top of the electric icebox.

Maisie's letter went along quietly enough for two paragraphs, listing the physical woes of herself and her family, a rather staggering list, to be sure, but containing nothing to cause my white hair to stand on end. And then came an alarming sentence.

"I tried to see you in December," she wrote, "but the timekeeper said you were in Florida."

This was the first news I had had that there is a man holding a watch on me. All my doom-shaped fears came back with a rush. It is true that I was not in Florida at the time, but this did not comfort me. I could only guess that the man who is watching the sands run through my hour-glass is not really on the job.

"What difference does it make where this bird is?" he probably says to himself. "He hasn't got many hours left, so why should I bother following him around? I'll just sit here and watch the clock."

There are times, however, when I think he *is* keeping track, that he is right in the room with me. Since I have, for the time being, about one-fiftieth vision, I can't actually see him; but I can hear him. It is no illusion that the blind become equipped with the eardrums of an elk hound. I can hear a pin drop on a carpet. It makes two sounds – a sharp plop when it strikes the carpet and a somewhat smaller sound, a faint thip! when it bounces and strikes again. It is because of acute sharpness of ear that I hear, or think I hear, the timekeeper. This is always when I am alone in a room, or think I am. I shut the radio off suddenly, and I hear him flitting across the carpet, making a sound about three times as loud as a pin.

"Hello," I say, but he never answers. Sometimes a waiter does, or a bell boy, or a maid who has crept into the room. On these occasions the timekeeper slips into a closet or under the bed. I never ask the waiter or the bell boy or the maid to look for the hiding man, for consider how it would sound. It would sound like this:

"Waiter?"

"Yes, sir?"

"Would you mind looking under the bed? I think there

is a timekeeper there."

"A timekeeper, sir? I'm sorry, sir, but it sounds as if you said timekeeper, sir."

"That's right – timekeeper. There is a timekeeper hiding somewhere in this room, a chap who wears sneakers, and a suit of the same design as the wallpaper, probably."

"I'm very sorry. Shall I call your doctor?"

"No, never mind, it's all right. Let it go."

I haven't let anybody call the doctor yet, but I am planning to let one of the waiters do it one of these days, a waiter named Heyst. He not only always brings the wrong order to me, but he is also the man who distributes the menus, shoving them under the door. To some people a menu being shoved under a door would make only a faint moving sound, but to me it sounds like a man stepping on a market basket, and is very disconcerting.

So I am going to let Heyst call the doctor some day. You know what would happen to a man who phoned a doctor and said, "The gentleman in 916 hears timekeepers, sir." He would be put away before sundown.

I don't know who pays the timekeeper. I do, probably, without knowing it – I can't see my checkbook stubs. It is thoughtful of him, at least, to carry a watch that makes no sound at all. That would keep me awake at night when he sits in a chair at the foot of my bed. Even the sound of a wrist-watch prevents me from sleeping, because it sounds like two men trying to take a wheel off a locomotive. If I put stopples in my ears, the racket is deadened somewhat. Then the ticking is fainter and farther away, a comparatively peaceful sound, like two men trying to take a rug away from a bulldog.

14

A GOOD MAN

It was about five years ago, just after my great-uncle, Mahlon Taylor, left Columbus, Ohio, to live in Punxsutawney, Pennsylvania, that I came across a faded obituary of my great-grandfather, Jacob Fisher, preserved in an old family scrapbook. Jacob, I learned, was born in 1808, one of the eleven children of Michael Fisher, who had built his cabin on the east shore of the Scioto River, south of Columbus, in 1799, the year George Washington died. Jacob Fisher's death notice, headed simply "Memorial", recorded that he was survived by three sisters and a brother, six of his thirteen children, thirty-two grand-children, and six great-grandchildren. The rest of the story, except for a single arresting sentence, praised the deceased's homely virtues – a persistent devotion to the Lord, kindliness to his neighbors, and generosity to those in want. The sentence that caught my eye and interest, set austerely apart in a paragraph by itself, read, "In his prime Jacob Fisher was the strongest man for many miles below the city." That was all; no instances were given of my great-grandfather's physical prowess. In the severe and solemn memorials of 1885 in Ohio there was no place for vain glorification of the pitiful and transitory clay. I wondered, when I read the obituary, what lay behind that cautious tribute to the earthly power of old Jake Fisher's flesh. It wasn't until I went to Columbus a month ago and met Mahlon Taylor, there on a visit too, that I found out.

A far lesser breed of men has succeeded the old gentleman on the American earth, and I tremble to think what he would have said of a great-grandson who turned out to be a writer. Perhaps I can make up for it a little by giving the substance of the story that should have followed that topic sentence left hanging mute and lonely in old Jake's obituary. He would have wanted it there in place of the list of his virtues.

Mahlon Taylor, a great-uncle of mine on my mother's side, is eighty-five years old, but he looks the same as he did when I last saw him, more than twenty years ago. He stands straight, walks spryly, and his mind and memory are as keen as his eyes, with which, without glasses, he can still see to shoot a rabbit or read a book. He has a thick head of white hair, on which people invariably compliment him. His secret is easy and inexpensive: for thirty years he has shampooed his head once a week with Old Dutch Cleanser. "I don't know what old Jake used," said Mahlon, "but his hair stayed full and black up to his death. Beard turned gray, but his hair didn't. He died with all his own teeth in his head, too – all except one.

That'd been knocked out with a brick in a fight."

Jake Fisher fought a thousand fights in his time. In those days, if you went west of the Alleghenies, there was only one way of settling an argument or a difference or opinion. Farther west they wrassled and gouged out eyes with their thumbnails, but in the Northwest Territory they fought standing up, with their fists. Some men would pick up a club or a rock or even a broadax and a few grabbed for their guns, but mostly they slugged it out toe to toe.

"Jake never lost a fight," Mahlon said. "He fought men who were hard on their womenfolks or were cruel to dumb animals, but mostly he fought to back up his political beliefs or to defend the divine inspiration of Scripture. 'There is too goddam much blasphemin' goes on,' he used to say. He was a good man."

Jacob Fisher, born in a log cabin when Jefferson was President, was twenty-one when Andrew Jackson took office. "Your great-grandpa's prime that the fella speaks of," said Uncle Mahlon, "began about then and lasted up to Cleveland's first term. He couldn't go through another Democratic administration, and so he died." Jake's political bias, it seems, was partly determined by an incident of the War of 1812. General Jackson had ordered the execution of a young soldier who had deserted to visit his dying mother. Jake heard about it from his father and he never got it out of his mind. He licked every Jackson man he met, once going up onto the platform of a meeting house to knock down a visiting speaker from the East who praised Old Hickory. Afterward he stopped his buggy beside the man, who was walking along the road, holding his jaw. "Git in the buggy and I'll take you to the hotel," said Jake. The man refused. "Git in the buggy!" roared Jake. The man got in. A fist fight settled an issue once and for all and subsequent hard feelings were not to be tolerated. If Jake broke a man's ribs or fractured his jaw, he took the man home. Often he sat up all night at the bedside of a vanquished foe, applying arnica or changing bandages. He could assist at the birth of a child and he had a comforting voice in a house of death. "About all the graves in the old Walnut Hill Cemetery were dug single-handed by Jake," said Uncle Mahlon. "He never allowed nobody to help him."

Jacob Fisher built one of the first stone houses south of Columbus, and people used to go out from the town to watch him pick up a 300-pound granite sill and set it in place. "He was only a hair over five foot ten," said Uncle Mahlon, "but he weighed a hundred and ninety-eight pounds, most of it bone and muscle. You couldn't lay your finger between his hipbone and his ribs, he was that close-built. He walked so straight he never run his shoes over, heel or sole – they wore out even." Around the house that Jake built grew up a farm of ten thousand acres. Through a part of his vast fields drifted the barges of the Ohio Canal on their way to and from Athens, and across one end of his property the Chillicothe tollpike was cut. Jake owned a great gravel pit and he allowed the road contractor to use all the gravel he needed, with the understanding that Jake would never have to pay toll. When the pike was finished and the tollgate put up, the agreement was forgotten. The pole would be kept in place across the road when Jake drove along in his buggy. "He'd git out and beat up the tollgate keeper," Uncle Mahlon told me, "and then raise the gate and drive on. They kept puttin' bigger and stronger men on the gate. Jake licked eight of 'em all told, and finally his patience gave out and he threatened to go over their heads to their bosses and lick *them*, and after that they didn't molest him. The gatekeeper would h'ist the gate when Jake's rig was still a quarter-mile away."

The canal wove itself into my great-grandfather's saga, too. If you stood on his back porch, you could see the slow boats passing through the land, half a mile away. Once in a while, when a barge came along, Jake would cup his hands around his mouth and bellow, "Git me some whiskey!" On the return trip five barrels would be tossed off onto Jake's land. He didn't drink or smoke or chew, but his hired hands did. When he was not yet forty, Jake had half a hundred Negroes working for him. Each man had a jug and a tin cup and the barrels were set in a lean-to and you could get whiskey whenever you wanted it. If a man got mean drunk or lazy drunk, Jake would whip him sober with a hickory withe. The men learned to drink moderately, out of fear of the big man's lash, and also out of a real devotion to him. "Your great-grandpa," said Uncle Mahlon, "was the first man in Franklin County to sit down at table with a Negro. This caused a stew and a fret in the Presbyterian church, but Jake just said, 'If a man's good enough to work for me, he's good enough to eat with me,' and that settled that."

One day there was hell and a battle royal along the canal.

Jake wandered down to the waterway and witnessed a dismaying spectacle. The bargemen were "whippin' up ducks". Each of the men held in his hand a long-lashed bullwhip. Their sport consisted of casting the whip at ducks floating in the canal in such a way that the far end of the lash wrapped itself several times about a duck's neck. Then they would jerk the bird up onto the barge. The bargemen were expert at this curious pastime. They caught a great many ducks. The ducks were Jake's. He ran down to the towpath, grabbed the tow-rope away from the drowsy boy on the mule, and hauled the boat into shore. Then he leaped on board and began to throw men into the water and onto the land. "He could throw a six-foot grown man as far as twenty-five feet when he was in a rage," said Uncle Mahlon. "A lot of heads cracked and bones broke that day, but nobody was killed. Your great-grandpa never tried to kill anybody – except one Indian. He was a good man."

I asked about the Indian. There were a great many Indians in Central Ohio in the first thirty years of Jake Fisher's prime, descendants, perhaps, of the braves, who fought at the Battle of Fallen Timbers. They plagued Jake because, although they couldn't outwrassle or outhoist him, they could outrun him. "If I could catch 'em," he used to say wistfully, "I could hold 'em." He never gave up trying. "Once, over by the old deer lick west of the river," Uncle Mahlon told me, "he challenged an Indian to a foot race – see which one could reach an old elm tree first. The Indian won by a couple of strides. Your great-grandpa ran back and got his gun where he had left it and shot the Indian. He wasn't killed, but he was hurt bad. Jake carried him to his own home and nursed him back to life. Old Fisher didn't get more than two, three hours' sleep a night for weeks, sittin' up with that Indian. The fella thought he was going to die, so he confessed to his sins and crimes, which included most of the thievin' and skulduggery that'd gone on in the county for the past five years. Your great-grandpa never gave him away to the authorities. Jake always said the Lord God Almighty disturbed his aim the day he shot that Indian."

Shortly after that, Jake became captain of a horse militia company, whose main duty was to keep order at public hangings. Captain Fisher, in his official capacity, wore a saber, but he never picked up a gun again, even to face an armed man. There was the November evening when Stambaugh showed up on the road outside the Fisher house. He was a quick-moving, broad-shouldered neighbor and there was bad blood between him and Milt Fisher, one of Jake's sons. It was suppertime and Jake had just finished saying grace. One of his darkies came running into the dining room. "Stambaugh's come to git Mr. Milt!" he said. "He got a shotgun in one hand and a broadax in t'other!" Jake told Milt and his other sons to sit still. He took his napkin out of his collar and went out the door, empty-handed. "Jake took Stambaugh's gun away from him and broke it in two," said Uncle Mahlon. "Then he snapped the ax handle and throwed the pieces away. He broke that gun and ax in his hands, like you'd break a stick."

*

When Fort Sumter was fired on, Jake Fisher, still hard as a boulder, had just turned fifty-three. They wouldn't take him in the Army, so he stayed at home and fought Copperheads and mealymouthed patriots with his fists. "On a market day Jake would lick as many as six, eight men," Uncle Mahlon said. "Mostly men who questioned Lincoln's policies or turned scared after a Rebel victory. Once a fella that was ridin' on a horse yelled something that angered your great-grandpa and Jake ordered him down off his horse. The fella was just takin' off his coat to square away when Jake walked over to the horse. "We gotta have more room," he said. "I don't want you to hit this horse when I throw you." Thereupon he picked the animal up in his arms and moved it eight or ten feet away. He was used to doing that in his own blacksmith shop – it was easier to move 'em that way than to lead 'em sometimes. Well, when the fella saw that he took to his heels and ran faster than an Indian."

On another occasion during the war years a friend of Jake's told him that five men, probably Copperheads, were conspiring to beat Jake up. They were in the back room of Frick's saloon, laying plans for a mass assault. Jake jumped on a horse and rode over to the place. "He didn't knock them fellas down," said Uncle Mahlon. "He throwed 'em. Jake only fought with his fists over political or religious questions. He throwed fellas that whipped up ducks or were just plain ornery." It was also during the Civil War, when Morgan's raiders had crossed over into Ohio, that a train of boxcars on its way to Cincinnati stopped in the yards in Columbus. Jake found out that they were crowded with men, Home Guards, on their way to protect the Ohio-Kentucky border. "The goddam Copperheads has cooped them boys up in there without no air!" said Jake. He tore a rail loose from a siding and, swinging it like a tennis racquet, beat holes in the sides of each car. The authorities always looked the other way when Jake started out on one of his rampages. "Nobody wanted to arrest a man as good as Jake," Uncle Mahlon said.

In his seventies, Jake Fisher could still lift two hundred pounds' dead weight from the ground and hold it at arm's length above his head. Three years before he died he performed his last exploit in public. The drunken driver of a team of horses on High Street tumbled over onto the doubletrees and the horses took off. Jake outran the other men who saw it happen and pulled the team to a stop. "I can still catch 'em," he said proudly, "and if I can catch 'em, I can hold 'em." In his last days he had little respect for the soft race of men he saw growing up around him. When he was taken to see a newborn great-grandchild, a puny boy weighing seven pounds, Jake snorted. "Goddam it," he said, "the next generation of Fishers is goin' to be squirrels."

In his seventy-seventh year, Jake took to his bed for the last time. As he lay dying, the preacher called on him. "Don't you want to forgive your enemies?" he asked. Jake smiled. "I ain't got none," he said. "I licked 'em all."

15

THE LETTERS OF JAMES THURBER

> Adams was a great letter writer of the type that is now almost
> extinct . . . his circle of friends was larger perhaps and more
> distinguished than that of any other American of his generation.
> — *H.S.Commager on "Letters of Henry Adams."*

James Thurber was a letter writer of the type that is now
completely extinct. His circle of correspondents was
perhaps no larger but it was easily more bewildered than
that of any other American of his generation. Thurber laid
the foundation for his voluminous correspondence during
his Formative Period. In those years he wrote to many
distinguished persons, none of whom ever replied, among
them Admiral Schley, Young Barbarian, Senator Atlee
Pomerene, June Caprice, and a man named Unglaub who
played first base for the Washington Senators at the turn of
the century. Unglaub, in Thurber's estimation, stood
head and shoulders above all the rest of his correspondents
and, indeed, he said so in his letter to McKinley. Thurber
did not write as many letters as Henry Adams or John Jay

Chapman or some of the other boys whose correspondence has been published lately, but that is because he never set pen to paper after his forty-third year.

The effect of Thurber's letters on his generation was about the same as the effect of anybody's letters on any generation; that is to say, nil. It is only when a man's letters are published after his death that they have any effect and this effect is usually only on literary critics. Nobody else ever reads a volume of letters and anybody who says he does is a liar. A person may pick up a volume of correspondence now and then and read a letter here and there, but he never gets any connected idea of what the man is trying to say and soon abandons the book for the poems of John Greenleaf Whittier. This is largely because every man whose letters have ever been published was in the habit of writing every third one to a Mrs. Cameron or a Mrs. Winslow or a Miss Betch, the confidante of a lifetime, with whom he shared any number of gaily obscure little secrets. These letters all read like this: "Dear Puttums: I love what you say about Mooey! It's so devastatingly true! B —— dropped in yesterday (Icky was out at the time) and gave some sort of report on Neddy but I am afraid I didn't listen (*ut ediendam aut debendo!*). He and Liddy are in Venice, I think I gathered, or Newport. What in the world do you suppose came over Buppa that Great Night??? You, of course, were as splendidly consequent as ever (*in loco sporenti abadabba est*) – but I was deeply disappointed in Sig's reaction. All he can think of, poor fellow, is Margery's 'flight'. Remind me to tell you some day what Pet said about the Ordeal." These particular letters are sometimes further obscured by a series of explanatory editorial footnotes, such as "Probably Harry Boynton or his brother Norton", "A neighbor at Bar Harbor", "The late Edward J.Belcher", "Also sometimes lovingly referred to as Butty, a niece-in-law by his first marriage". In the end, as I say, one lays the book aside for "Snow-Bound" in order to get a feeling of reality before going to bed.

Thurber's letters from Europe during his long stay there in 1937 and 1938 (the European Phase) are perhaps the least interesting of all those he, or anybody else, ever wrote. He seems to have had at no time any idea at all, either clear or vague, as to what was going on. A certain Groping, to be sure, is discernible, but it doesn't appear to be toward anything. All this may have been due in great part to the fact that he took his automobile to Europe with him and spent most of his time worrying about running out of gas. The gasoline gauge of his car had got out of order and sometimes registered "empty" when the tank was half full and "full" when it contained only two or three gallons. A stronger character would have had the gauge fixed or carried a five-gallon can of *essence* in the back of the car, thus releasing the mind for more mature and significant preoccupations, but not Thurber.

I have been unable to find any one of Thurber's many correspondents who saved any of his letters (Thurber himself kept carbons, although this is not generally known or cared about). "We threw them out when we moved," people would tell me, or "We gave them to the janitor's little boy." Thurber gradually became aware of this on his return to America (the Final Phase) because of the embarrassed silence that always greeted him when, at his friends' homes, he would say, "Why don't we get out my letters to you and read them aloud?" After a painful pause the subject was quickly changed, usually by putting up the ping-pong table.

In his last years the once voluminous letter writer ceased writing letters altogether, and such communication as he maintained with the great figures of his time was over the telephone and consisted of getting prominent persons on the phone, making a deplorable sound with his lips, and hanging up. His continual but vain attempts to reach the former Barbara Hutton by phone clouded the last years of his life but at the same time gave him something to do. His last words, to his wife, at the fag end of the Final Phase, were "Before they put up the ping-pong table, tell them I am not running out of gas." He was as wrong, and as mixed up, in this particular instance as he was in most others. I am not sure that we should not judge him too harshly.

16

A FRIEND TO ALEXANDER

"I have taken to dreaming about Aaron Burr every night,"
Andrews said.

"What for?" said Mrs. Andrews.

"How do I know what for?" Andrews snarled. "What
for, the woman says."

Mrs. Andrews did not flare up; she simply looked at her
husband as he lay on the chaise longue in her bedroom in
his heavy blue dressing gown, smoking a cigarette.
Although he had just got out of bed, he looked haggard
and tired. He kept biting his lower lip between puffs.

"Aaron Burr is a funny person to be dreaming about
nowadays – I mean with all the countries in the world at
war with each other. I wish you would go and see Dr.
Fox," said Mrs. Andrews, taking her thumb from
between the pages of her mystery novel and tossing the
book toward the foot of the bed. She sat up straighter
against her pillow. "Maybe haliver oil or B_1 is what you
need," she said. "B_1 does wonders for people. I don't see

why you see *him* in your dreams. *Where* do you see him?"

"Oh, places; in Washington Square or Bowling Green or on Broadway. I'll be talking to a woman in a victoria, a woman holding a white lace parasol, and suddenly there will be Burr, bowing and smiling and smelling like a carnation, telling his stories about France and getting off his insults."

Mrs. Andrews lighted a cigarette, although she rarely smoked until after lunch. "Who is the woman in the victoria?" she asked.

"What? How do I know? You know about people in dreams, don't you? They are nobody at all, or everybody."

"You see Aaron Burr plainly enough, though. I mean he isn't nobody or everybody."

"All right, all right," said Andrews. "You have me there. But I don't know who the woman is, and I don't care. Maybe it's Madame Jumel or Mittens Willett or a girl I knew in high school. That's not important."

"Who is Mittens Willett?" asked Mrs. Andrews.

"She was a famous New York actress in her day, fifty years ago or so. She's buried in an old cemetery on Second Avenue."

"That's very sad," said Mrs. Andrews.

"Why is it?" demanded Andrews, who was now pacing up and down the deep-red carpet.

"I mean she probably died young," said Mrs. Andrews. "Almost all women did in those days."

Andrews ignored her and walked over to a window and looked out at a neat, bleak street in the Fifties. "He's a vile, cynical cad," said Andrews, suddenly turning away from the window. "I was standing talking to Alexander Hamilton when Burr stepped up and slapped him in the face. When I looked at Hamilton, who do you suppose he was?"

"I don't know," said Mrs. Andrews. "Who was he?"

"He was my brother, the one I've told you about, the one who was killed by that drunkard in the cemetery."

Mrs. Andrews had never got that story straight and she didn't want to go into it again now; the facts in the tragic case and her way of getting them mixed up always drove Andrews into a white-faced fury. "I don't think we ought to dwell on our nightmare," said Mrs. Andrews. "I think we ought to get out more. We could go to the country for weekends."

Andrews wasn't listening; he was back at the window, staring out into the street again.

"I wish he'd go back to France and stay there," Andrews snapped out suddenly the next morning at breakfast.

"Who, dear?" said his wife. "Oh, you mean Aaron Burr. Did you dream about him again? I don't see why you dream about him all the time. Don't you think you ought to take some Luminal?"

"No," said Andrews. "I don't know. Last night he kept shoving Alexander around."

"Alexander?"

"Hamilton. God knows I'm familiar enough with him to call him by his first name. He hides behind my coat-tails every night, or tries to."

"I was thinking we might go to the Old Drovers' Inn this weekend," said Mrs. Andrews. "You like it there."

"Hamilton has become not only my brother Walter but practically every other guy I have ever liked," said Andrews. "That's natural."

"Of course it is," she said. They got up from the table. "I do wish you'd go to Dr. Fox."

"I'm going to the Zoo," he said, "and feed popcorn to the rhinoceros. That makes things seem right, for a little while anyway."

It was two nights later at five o'clock in the morning that Andrews bumbled into his wife's bedroom in pajamas and bare feet, his hair in his eyes, his eyes wild. "He got him!" he croaked. "He got him! The bastard got him. Alexander fired into the air, he fired in the air and smiled at him, just like Walter, and that fiend from hell took deliberate aim – I saw him – I saw him take deliberate aim – he killed him in cold blood, the foul scum!"

Mrs. Andrews, not quite awake, was fumbling in the box containing the Nembutal while her husband ranted on. She made him take two of the little capsules, between his sobs.

Andrews didn't want to go to see Dr. Fox but he went to humor his wife. Dr. Fox leaned back in his swivel chair behind his desk and looked at Andrews. "Now, just what seems to be the trouble?" he asked.

"Nothing seems to be the trouble," said Andrews.

The doctor looked at Mrs. Andrews. "He has night-mares," she said.

"You look a little underweight, perhaps," said the doctor. "Are you eating well, getting enough exercise?"

"I'm not underweight," said Andrews. "I eat the way I always have and get the same exercise."

At this, Mrs. Andrews sat straighter in her chair and began to talk, while her husband lighted a cigarette. "You see, I think he's worried about something," she said, "because he always has this same dream. It's about his brother Walter, who was killed in a cemetery by a drunken man, only it isn't *really* about him."

The doctor did the best he could with this information. He cleared his throat, tapped on the glass top of his desk with the fingers of his right hand, and said, "Very few people are actually *killed* in cemeteries." Andrews stared at the doctor coldly and said nothing. "I wonder if you would mind stepping into the next room," the doctor said to him.

"Well, I hope you're satisfied," Andrews snapped at his wife as they left the doctor's office a half-hour later. "You heard what he said. There's nothing the matter with me at all."

"I'm glad your heart is so fine," she told him. "He said it was fine, you know."

"Sure," said Andrews. "It's fine. Everything's fine." They got into a cab and drove home in silence.

"I was just thinking," said Mrs. Andrews, as the cab stopped in front of their apartment building, "I was just thinking that now that Alexander Hamilton is dead, you won't see anything more of Aaron Burr." The cab-driver, who was handing Andrews change for a dollar bill, dropped a quarter on the floor.

Mrs. Andrews was wrong. Aaron Burr did not depart from her husband's dreams. Andrews said nothing about it for several mornings, but she could tell. He brooded over his breakfast, did not answer any of her questions, and jumped in his chair if she dropped a knife or spoon. "Are you still dreaming about that man?" she asked him finally.

"I wish I hadn't told you about it," he said. "Forget it, will you?"

"I can't forget it with you going on this way," she said. "I think you ought to see a psychiatrist. What does he do now?"

"What does who do now?" Andrews asked.

"Aaron Burr," she said. "I don't see why he keeps coming into your dreams now."

Andrews finished his coffee and stood up. "He goes around bragging that he did it with his eyes closed," he snarled. "He says he didn't even look. He claims he can hit the ace of spades at thirty paces blindfolded. Furthermore, since you asked what he does, he jostles me at parties now."

Mrs. Andrews stood up too and put her hand on her husband's shoulder. "I think you should stay out of this, Harry," she said. "It wasn't any business of yours, anyway, and it happened so long ago."

"I'm not getting into anything," said Andrews, his voice rising to a shout. "It's getting into me. Can't you see that?"

"I see that I've got to get you away from here," she said. "Maybe if you slept someplace else for a few nights, you wouldn't dream about him any more. Let's go to the country tomorrow. Let's go to the Lime Rock Lodge."

Andrews stood for a long while without answering her. "Why can't we go and visit the Crowleys?" he said finally. "They live in the country. Bob has a pistol and we could do a little target-shooting."

"What do you want to shoot a pistol for?" she asked quickly. "I should think you'd want to get away from that."

"Yeh," he said, "sure," and there was a far-off look in his eyes. "Sure."

When they drove into the driveway of the Crowleys' house, several miles north of New Milford, late the next afternoon, Andrews was whistling "Bye-Bye, Blackbird." Mrs. Andrews sighed contentedly and then, as her husband stopped the car, she began looking around wildly. "My bag!" she cried. "Did I forget to bring my bag?" He laughed his old, normal laugh for the first time in many days as he found the bag and handed it to her, and then, for the first time in many days, he leaned over and kissed her.

The Crowleys came out of the house and engulfed their guests in questions and exclamations. "How you been?" said Bob Crowley to Andrews, heartily putting an arm around his shoulder.

"Never better," said Andrews, "never better. Boy, it is good to be here!"

They were swept into the house to a shakerful of Bob Crowley's icy Martinis. Mrs. Andrews stole a happy glance over the edge of her glass at her husband's relaxed face.

When Mrs. Andrews awoke the next morning, her husband lay rigidly on his back in the bed next to hers, staring at the ceiling. "Oh, God," said Mrs. Andrews.

Andrews didn't move his head. "One Henry Andrews, an architect," he said suddenly in a mocking tone. "One Henry Andrews, an architect."

"What's the matter, Harry?" she asked. "Why don't you go back to sleep? It's only eight o'clock."

"That's what he calls me!" shouted Andrews. " 'One Henry Andrews, an architect,' he keeps saying in his nasty little sneering voice. 'One Henry Andrews, an architect.' "

"Please don't yell!" said Mrs. Andrews. "You'll wake the whole house. It's early. People want to sleep."

Andrews lowered his voice a little. "I'm beneath him," he snarled. "I'm just anybody. I'm a man in a gray suit. 'Be on your good behavior, my good man,' he says to me, 'or I shall have one of my lackeys give you a taste of the riding crop.' "

Mrs. Andrews sat up in bed. "Why should he say that to you?" she asked. "He wasn't such a great man, was he? I mean, didn't he try to sell Louisiana to the French, or something, behind Washington's back?"

"He was a scoundrel," said Andrews, "but a very brilliant mind."

Mrs. Andrews lay down again. "I was in hopes you

weren't going to dream about him any more," she said. "I thought if I brought you up here – "

"It's him or me," said Andrews grimly. "I can't stand this forever."

"Neither can I," Mrs. Andrews said, and there was a hint of tears in her voice.

Andrews and his host spent most of the afternoon, as Mrs. Andrews had expected, shooting at targets on the edge of the wood behind the Crowley studio. After the first few rounds, Andrews surprised Crowley by standing with his back to the huge hulk of dead tree trunk on which the targets were nailed, walking thirty paces ahead in a stiff-legged, stern-faced manner, with his revolver held at arm's length above his head, then turning suddenly and firing.

Crowley dropped to the ground, uninjured but scared. "What the hell's the big idea, Harry?" he yelled.

Andrews didn't say anything, but started to walk back to the tree again. Once more he stood with his back to the target and began stepping off the thirty paces.

"I think they kept their arm hanging straight down," Bob called to him. "I don't think they stuck it up in the air."

Andrews, still counting to himself, lowered his arm, and this time, as he turned at the thirtieth step, he whirled and fired from his hip, three times in rapid succession.

"Hey!" said Crowley.

Two of the shots missed the tree but the last one hit it, about two feet under the target. Crowley looked at his house guest oddly as Andrews began to walk back to the tree again, without a word, his lips tight, his eyes bright, his breath coming fast.

"What the hell?" Crowley said to himself. "Look, it's my turn," he called, but Andrews turned, then stalked ahead, unheeding. This time when he wheeled and fired, his eyes were closed.

"Good God Almighty, man!" said Crowley from the grass, where he lay flat on his stomach. "Hey, give me that gun, will you?" he demanded, getting to his feet.

Andrews let him take it. "I need a lot more practice, I guess," he said.

"Not with me standing around," said Crowley. "Come on, let's go back to the house and shake up a drink. I've got the jumps."

"I need a lot more practice," said Andrews again.

He got his practice next morning just as the sun came up and the light was hard and the air was cold. He had crawled softly out of bed, dressed silently, and crept out of the room. He knew where Crowley kept the target pistol and the cartridges. There would be a target on the tree trunk, just as high as a man's heart. Mrs. Andrews heard the shots first and sat sharply upright in bed, crying "Harry!" almost before she was awake. Then she heard more shots. She got up, put on a dressing gown, and went to the Crowleys' door. She heard them moving about in their room. Alice opened the door and stepped out into the hall when Mrs. Andrews knocked. "Is Harry all right?" asked Mrs. Andrews. "Where is he? What is he doing?"

"He's out shooting behind the studio, Bob says," Alice told her. "Bob'll go out and get him. Maybe he had a nightmare, or walked in his sleep."

"No," said Mrs. Andrews, "he never walks in his sleep. He's awake."

"Let's go down and put on some coffee," said Alice. "He'll need some."

Crowley came out of the bedroom and joined the women in the hallway. "I'll need some too," he said. "Good morning, Bess. I'll bring him back. What the hell's the matter with him, anyway?" He was down the stairs and gone before she could answer. She was glad of that.

"Come on," said Alice, taking her arm. They went down to the kitchen.

Mrs. Crowley found the butler in the kitchen, just standing there. "It's all right, Madison," she said. "You go back to bed. Tell Clotheta it's all right. Mr. Andrews is just shooting a little. He couldn't sleep."

"Yes, Ma'am," mumbled Madison, and went back to tell his wife that they said it was all right.

"It can't be right," said Clotheta, "Shootin' pistols at this time of night."

"Hush up," Madison told her. He was shivering as he climbed back into bed.

"I wish dat man would go 'way from heah," grumbled Clotheta. "He's got a bad look to his eyes."

Andrews brightened Clotheta's life by going away late that afternoon. When he and his wife got in their car and drove off, the Crowleys slumped into chairs and looked at each other and said, "Well." Crowley got up finally to mix a drink. "What do you think is the matter with Harry?" he asked.

"I don't know," said his wife. "It's what Clotheta would call the shoots, I suppose."

"He said a funny thing when I went out and got him this morning," Crowley told her.

"I could stand a funny thing," she said.

"I asked him what the hell he was doing there in that freezing air with only his pants and shirt and shoes on. 'I'll get him one of these nights,' he said."

"Why don't you sleep in my room tonight?" Mrs. Andrews asked her husband as he finished his Scotch-and-water nightcap.

"You'd keep shaking me all night to keep me awake," he said. "You're afraid to let me meet him. Why do you always think everybody else is better than I am? I can outshoot him the best day he ever lived. Furthermore, I have a modern pistol. He has to use an old-fashioned single-shot muzzle-loader." Andrews laughed nastily.

"Is that quite fair?" his wife asked after a moment of thoughtful silence.

He jumped up from his chair. "What do I care if it's fair or not?" he snarled.

She got up too. "Don't be mad with me, Harry," she said. There were tears in her eyes.

"I'm sorry, darling," he said, taking her in his arms.

"I'm very unhappy," she sobbed.

"I'm sorry, darling," he said again. "Don't you worry about me. I'll be all right. I'll be fine." She was crying too wildly to say anything more.

When she kissed him good night later on she knew it was really good-bye. Women have a way of telling when you aren't coming back.

"Extraordinary," said Dr. Fox the next morning, letting Andrews' dead left hand fall back upon the bed. "His heart was as sound as a dollar when I examined him the other day. It has just stopped as if he had been shot."

Mrs. Andrews, through her tears, was looking at her dead husband's right hand. The three fingers next to the index finger were closed in stiffly on the palm, as if gripping the handle of a pistol. The taut thumb was doing its part to hold that invisible handle tightly and unwaveringly. But it was the index finger that Mrs. Andrews' eyes stayed on longest. It was only slightly curved inward, as if it were just about to press the trigger of the pistol. "Harry never even fired a shot," wailed Mrs. Andrews. "Aaron Burr killed him the way he killed Hamilton. Aaron Burr shot him through the heart. I knew he would. I knew he would."

Dr. Fox put an arm about the hysterical woman and led her from the room. "She is crazy," he said to himself. "Stark, raving crazy."

17

THE VENGEANCE OF 3902090

I believe it was the late Hart Crane who once said, at a meeting of literary persons, "We are all trapped!" A few of the more neurotic lady authors made for the door, under the impression that the place was on fire, but most of the male writers stood their ground and nodded their heads in rueful agreement. They comprehended what he meant: we are trapped in consciousness, trapped by mortality, trapped inside an inadequate animal body, trapped within the poor limitations of the human spirit. Some of us (this is what I have been leading up to) also happen to be caught in smaller prisons within the larger ones, like a mouse in a trap in Sing Sing. This type of badgered human being is given to the short, nervous essay rather than to the 972-page novel or autobiography. He is more likely to fret about the discomforts of his particular cell than to concern himself with prison problems as a whole. You will find him in bed groaning when other people are up lecturing. This frailty, this preoccupation with, and affinity for, the smaller enormities of life, permits him to be overwhelmed by minor tyrannies and persecutions to the extent that, for days on end, he forgets his part in the struggle for that larger Freedom which now engages the attention of all right-minded prisoners of the world. I happen to be intensely dedicated to opposing the perilous wrongs and injustices of this bad earth, but right at the moment all I can worry about is my troubles as No. 3902090.

The sovereign State of Connecticut long ago laid a pretty trap for me. For years, like a fox, I avoided it, but this year it clamped down on me one lovely afternoon in Lakeville. In Connecticut I am motor-vehicle operator No. 3902090. Whenever Connecticut thinks of me, she thinks of me as that. Our relations, until recently, have been friendly but statistical. I don't suppose now that I shall go back to her, although we may have lunch together once in a while in one of those lovely old inns. I'll say this for her, she has lovely old inns. But to get back to the trouble that came between us. Each year, before midnight on the last day of February, I must send in my application for renewal of my passenger vehicle registration. I can say, in all honesty, that I have never kept her waiting; she has always got my seven dollars long before it was due. Every time that I sent it in, however, it was my natural tendency, and great desire, to enclose in the same envelope my application for renewal of my driver's license, together with the three dollars demanded for that. But no. I am not allowed to. I am not allowed to send *that* in before March 20th (as arbitrary and unmemorable a date as August 17th or February 11th). I do not know how Connecticut excuses this fiscal dowdiness; all I know is that I look upon it as a trap.

I have built up a rude mental picture of a fat gentleman with thinning hair and octagonal glasses whom no motorist has ever heard of or ever seen, a Goebbels of red tape, a Göring for discipline. He sits up in Hartford and, at the beginning of every year, says to his secretary, "We will trap old 3902090 *this* time, my girl! He'll get his plates and his passenger registration and then he'll go through our compulsory semi-annual inspection of his vehicle and get several more pieces of paper – one to paste on his windshield – and by the time March twentieth comes around he'll think he has all the documents necessary to drive a car; he'll forget to send in that little yellow slip for renewal of his driver's license. After all, it's only four and a quarter by two and a half inches in size, and 3902090 has been known to mislay a card table. Once he sent in his application for driver's license too early and we shot it right back at him. Thought we had him that year, thought he'd forget to send it in again – kind of subconsciously thinking he'd already done it, see? But he fooled us. He'll forget it this time, though – got a lot of worries, I hear; and he won't see the warnings in the newspapers because his eyes have gone back on him and he can't read anything except children's books with large colored type. Oh, we'll get him, my girl! I've always wanted to slap one on old 3902090, he thinks he's so smart; hasn't been caught in ten years. But we'll get him." They got me.

There isn't any use going into the argument with the state policeman who sprang the trap on me. You know it by heart. He was, my wife said, a very handsome fellow. All I know is that he was big and inflexible and wore a pretty uniform. I am against state policemen wearing uniforms, especially good-looking state policemen wearing good-looking uniforms. It gives them a sense of well-groomed power, it brings that jaunty I-could-jail-you-for-life-for-this-buddy tone into their voice. I want to see them all in three-button sack suits with soiled gray felt hats. A man with so much authority should start out after his prey under the handicap of looking a little funny, a little unimportant. It would lend him the great and rare blessing of humility. (If I could think of even one plain-clothesman who was humble, I would feel more confident about this.)

All these ideas, of course, I thought up later. The state trooper gave me the works, and I just snarled a little. He pointed out that my 1938 driver's license had expired two days before. He said he imagined several other troopers would hold me up before I got home and each give me a summons – all of them for different courts. I drove off with my summons and I began to dream of a little home in Vermont. It was plain that Connecticut didn't love me, or she wouldn't want to prosecute me in every court from Waterbury to Lakeville for my poor little first offense (into which, as you now know, I was trapped). When I went to bed that night (he was just trying to scare me about those other cops), I said some telling things to him. I said, "I *have* a license to drive this car, which I got by passing a rigorous test. (It wasn't really rigorous.) You hold that license in your hand. I have simply forgot to renew it. My only fault is that I owe the State of Connecticut three dollars." Then I went into a bitter arraignment of a state which makes you pay for your car in February but won't let you pay for the right to drive it till March. I waxed what could easily be called eloquent. I think it was at this moment that I coined the expression "fiscal dowdiness." I am rather glad now I didn't think of it and use it when I was actually talking to the trooper. I might be in the Lakeville jail; or I might have a broken jaw.

I am by no means going to let the whole thing drop. I have thought up a nice little scheme for revenge. The day after I was held up, I drove over to Hartford by side roads – disguised as an Ohioan – and got my 1939 driver's license. Attached to it, as always, is an application blank for next year's license ("Mail this application on or after March 20, 1940"). I found, in examining the license very carefully, this remarkable message: "You must notify this department if you have suffered any physical or mental infirmity during the past year if it interferes with the operation of a motor vehicle." My plan is a simple but fiendish one. I am going to write the Man in Hartford a note, scrawled but legible. "Dear Sir," I shall say, "Since I got my 1939 operator's license I have gone nuts. I am as crazy as a monkey and am letting you know, like you asked. I am going to lay for you and run you down. There is no use in your trying to escape me. If you notify the police, I will run down your secretary. Every time you see a red light, drop $5,000 out of your car in a shoe box; the money must all be in three-dollar bills." I am going to sign it, quite simply, "3902090". I suppose they will catch up with me in the end, but it will be fun. It is fun already. I spend a great deal of time imagining the Man in Hartford opening my note, turning pale, grabbing a chair for support, and saying to his secretary, "Good God, girl, 3902090 has got us!"

Now maybe I can give some of my energies to the struggle for that larger Freedom which engages the attention of all right-minded prisoners of the world.

18

THE STORY OF SAILING

People who visit you in Bermuda are likely to notice, even before they notice the flowers of the island, the scores of sailing craft which fleck the harbors and the ocean round about. Furthermore, they are likely to ask you about the ships before they ask you about the flowers and this, at least in my own case, is unfortunate, because although I know practically nothing about flowers I know ten times as much about flowers as I know about ships. Or at any rate I did before I began to study up on the subject. Now I feel that I am pretty well qualified to hold my own in any average discussion of rigging.

I began to brush up on the mysteries of sailing a boat after an unfortunate evening when a lady who sat next to me at dinner turned to me and said, "Do you reef in your gaff-topsails when you are close-hauled or do you let go the mizzen-top-bowlines and cross-jack-braces?" She took me for a sailor and not a landlubber and of course I hadn't the slightest idea what she was talking about.

One reason for this was that none of the principal words (except "reef") used in the sentence I have quoted is pronounced the way it is spelled: "gaff-topsails" is pronounced "gassles", "close-hauled" is pronounced "cold", "mizzen-top-bowlines" is pronounced "mittens", and "cross-jack-braces" is pronounced "crabapples" or something that sounds a whole lot like that. Thus what the lady really said to me was, "Do you reef in your gassles when you are cold or do you let go the mittens and crabapples?" Many a visitor who is asked such a question takes the first ship back home, and it is for these embarrassed gentlemen that I am going to explain briefly the history and terminology of sailing.

In the first place, there is no doubt but that the rigging of the modern sailing ship has become complicated beyond all necessity. If you want proof of this you have only to look up the word "rigging" in the Encyclopædia Britannica. You will find a drawing of a full-rigged modern ship and under it an explanation of its various spars, masts, sails, etc. There are forty-five different major parts, beginning with "bowsprit" and going on up to "davit topping-lifts." Included in between are, among others, these items: the fore-top-mast staysail halliards (pron. "fazzles"), the topgallant mast-yard-and-lift (pron. "toft"), the mizzen-topgallant-braces (pron. "maces"), and the fore-topmast backstays and top-sail tye (pron. "frassantossle"). The tendency of the average landlubber who studies this diagram for five minutes is to turn to "Sanscrit" in the encyclopaedia and study up on that instead, but only a coward would do that. It is possible to get something out of the article on rigging if you keep at it long enough.

Let us creep up on the formidable modern sailing ship in our stocking feet, beginning with one of the simplest of all known sailing craft, the Norse Herring Boat. Now when the Norse built their sailing boats they had only one idea in mind: to catch herring. They were pretty busy men, always a trifle chilly, and they had neither the time nor the inclination to sit around on the cold decks of their ships trying to figure out all the different kinds of ropes, spars, and sails that might be hung on their masts. Each ship had, as a matter of fact, only one mast. Near the top of it was a cross-piece of wood and on that was hung one simple square sail, no more complicated than the awning of a cigar store. A rope was attached to each end of the cross-piece and the other ends of these ropes were held by the helmsman. By manipulating the ropes he could make the ship go ahead, turn right, or turn left. It was practically impossible to make it turn around, to be sure, and that is the reason the Norsemen went straight on and discovered America, thus proving that it isn't really necessary to turn around.

As the years went on and the younger generations of Norsemen became, like all younger generations, less hard-working and more restless than their forebears, they began to think less about catching herring and more about monkeying with the sails of their ships. One of these restless young Norsemen one day lengthened the mast of his ship, put up another cross-piece about six feet above the first one, and hung another but smaller sail on his new cross-piece, or spar (pronounced, strange as it may seem, "spar"). Thus was the main topsail born.

After that, innovations in sails followed so fast that the herring boat became a veritable shambles of canvas. A Norseman named Leif the Sailmaker added a second mast to his ship, just in front of the first one, and thus the foremast came into being and with it the fore mainsail and the fore topsail. A Turk named Skvar added a third mast and called it the mizzen. Not to be outdone, a Muscovite named Amir put up a third spar on each of his masts; Skvar put up a fourth; Amir replied with a fifth; Skvar came back with a sixth, and so it went, resulting in the topgallant foresail, the top-topgallant mizzen sail, the top-top-topgallant main topsail, and the tip-top-topgallant-gallant mainsail (pron. "twee twee twee twa twa").

Practically nobody today sails a full-rigged seven-masted ship, so that it would not be especially helpful to describe in detail all the thousands of different gaffs, sprits, queeps, weems, lugs, miggets, loords (spelled "leewards"), gessels, grommets, etc., on such a ship. I shall therefore devote what space I have left to a discussion of how to come back alive from a pleasant sail in the ordinary twenty- or thirty-foot sailing craft such as you are likely to be "taken for a ride" in down in Bermuda. This type of so-called pleasure ship is not only given to riding on its side, due to coming about without the helmsman's volition (spelled "jibe" and pronounced "look out, here we go again!"), but it is made extremely perilous by what is known as the flying jib, or boom.

The boom is worse than the gaff for some people can

stand the gaff (hence the common expression "he can stand the gaff") but nobody can stand the boom when it aims one at him from the floor. With the disappearance of the Norse herring fisherman and the advent of the modern pleasure craft sailor, the boom became longer and heavier and faster. Helmsmen will tell you that they keep swinging the boom across the deck of the ship in order to take advantage of the wind but after weeks of observation it is my opinion that they do it to take advantage of the passengers. The only way to avoid the boom and have any safety at all while sailing is to lie flat on your stomach in the bottom of the ship. This is very uncomfortable on account of the hard boards and because you can't see a thing, but it is the one sure way I know of to go sailing and come back in the boat and not be washed up in the surf. I recommend the posture highly, but not as highly as I recommend the bicycle. My sailing adventures in Bermuda have made me appreciate for the first time the essential wonder of the simple, boomless bicycle.

19

HERE LIES MISS GROBY

Miss Groby taught me English composition thirty years ago. It wasn't what prose said that interested Miss Groby; it was the way prose said it. The shape of a sentence crucified on a blackboard (parsed, she called it) brought a light to her eye. She hunted for Topic Sentences and Transitional Sentences the way little girls hunt for white violets in springtime. What she loved most of all were Figures of Speech. You remember her. You must have had her, too. Her influence will never die out of the land. A small schoolgirl asked me the other day if I could give her an example of metonymy. (There are several kinds of metonymies, you may recall, but the one that will come to mind most easily, I think, is Container for the Thing Contained.) The vision of Miss Groby came clearly before me when the little girl mentioned the old, familiar word. I saw her sitting at her desk, taking the rubber band off the roll-call cards, running it back upon the fingers of her right hand, and surveying us all separately with quick little henlike turns of her head.

Here lies Miss Groby, not dead, I think, but put away on a shelf with the other T squares and rulers whose edges had lost their certainty. The fierce light that Miss Groby brought to English literature was the light of Identification. Perhaps, at the end, she could no longer retain the dates of the birth and death of one of the Lake poets. That would have sent her to the principal of the school with her resignation. Or perhaps she could not remember, finally, exactly how many Cornishmen there were who had sworn that Trelawny should not die, or precisely how many springs were left to Housman's lad in which to go about the woodlands to see the cherry hung with snow.

Verse was one of Miss Groby's delights because there was so much in both its form and content that could be counted. I believe she would have got an enormous thrill out of Wordsworth's famous lines about Lucy if they had been written this way:

> A violet by a mossy stone
> Half hidden from the eye,
> Fair as a star when ninety-eight
> Are shining in the sky.

It is hard for me to believe that Miss Groby ever saw any famous work of literature from far enough away to know what it meant. She was forever climbing up the margins of books and crawling between their lines, hunting for the little gold of phrase, making marks with a pencil. As Palamides hunted the Questing Beast, she hunted the Figure of Speech. She hunted it through the clangorous halls of Shakespeare and through the green forests of Scott.

Night after night, for homework, Miss Groby set us to searching in "Ivanhoe" and "Julius Caesar" for metaphors, similes, metonymies, apostrophes, personifications, and all the rest. It got so that figures of speech jumped out of the pages at you, obscuring the sense and pattern of the novel or play you were trying to read. "Friends, Romans, countrymen, lend me your ears." Take that, for instance. There is an unusual but perfect example of Container for the Thing Contained. If you read the funeral oration unwarily – that is to say, for its meaning – you might easily miss the C.F.T.T.C. Antony is, of course, not asking for their ears in the sense that he wants them cut off and handed over; he is asking for the function of those ears, for their power to hear, for, in a word, the thing they contain.

At first I began to fear that all the characters in Shakespeare and Scott were crazy. They confused cause with effect, the sign for the thing signified, the thing held for the thing holding it. But after a while I began to suspect that it was I myself who was crazy. I would find myself lying awake at night saying over and over, "The thinger for the thing contained". In a great but probably misguided attempt to keep my mind on its hinges, I would stare at the ceiling and try to think of an example of the Thing Contained for the Container. It struck me as odd that Miss Groby had never thought of that inversion. I finally hit on one, which I still remember. If a woman were to grab up a bottle of Grade A and say to her husband,

"Get away from me or I'll hit you with the milk", that would be a Thing Contained for the Container. The next day in class I raised my hand and brought my curious discovery straight out before Miss Groby and my astonished schoolmates. I was eager and serious about it and it never occurred to me that the other children would laugh. They laughed loudly and long. When Miss Groby had quieted them she said to me rather coldly, "That was not really amusing, James." That's the mixed-up kind of thing that happened to me in my teens.

In later years I came across another excellent example of this figure of speech in a joke long since familiar to people who know vaudeville or burlesque (or radio, for that matter). It goes something like this:

> A: What's your head all bandaged up for?
> B: I got hit with some tomatoes.
> A: How could that bruise you up so bad?
> B: These tomatoes were in a can.

I wonder what Miss Groby would have thought of that one.

I dream of my old English teacher occasionally. It seems that we are always in Sherwood Forest and that from far away I can hear Robin Hood winding his silver horn.

"Drat that man for making such a racket on his cornet!" cries Miss Groby. "He scared away a perfectly darling Container for the Thing Contained, a great, big, beautiful one. It leaped right back into its context when that man blew that cornet. It was the most wonderful Container for the Thing Contained I ever saw here in the Forest of Arden."

"This is Sherwood Forest," I say to her.

"That doesn't make any difference at all that I can see," she says to me.

Then I wake up, tossing and moaning.

20

A SORT OF GENIUS

On the morning of Saturday the 16th of September, 1922, a boy named Raymond Schneider and a girl named Pearl Bahmer, walking down a lonely lane on the outskirts of New Brunswick, New Jersey, came upon something that made them rush to the nearest house in Easton Avenue, around the corner, shouting. In that house an excited woman named Grace Edwards listened to them wide-eyed and then telephoned the police. The police came on the run and examined the young people's discovery: the bodies of a man and woman. They had been shot to death and the woman's throat was cut. Leaning against one of the man's shoes was his calling card, not as if it had fallen there but as if it had been placed there. It bore the name Rev. Edward W. Hall. He had been the rector of the Protestant Episcopal Church of St. John the Evangelist in New Brunswick. The woman was identified as Mrs. Eleanor R. Mills, wife of the sexton of that church. Raymond Schneider and Pearl Bahmer had stumbled upon what was to go down finally in the annals of our crime as perhaps the country's most remarkable mystery. Nobody was ever found guilty of the murders. Before the case was officially closed, a hundred and fifty persons had had their day in court and on the front pages of the newspapers. The names of two must already have sprung to your mind: Mrs. Jane Gibson, called by the avid press "the pig woman", and William Carpender Stevens, once known to a hundred million people simply as "Willie". The pig woman died eleven years ago, but Willie Stevens is alive. He still lives in the house that he lived in fourteen years ago with Mr. and Mrs. Hall, at 23 Nichol Avenue, New Brunswick.

It was from that house that the Rev. Mr. Hall walked at around 7:30 o'clock on the night of Thursday the 14th of September, 1922, to his peculiar doom. With the activities in that house after Mr. Hall's departure the State of New Jersey was to be vitally concerned. No. 23 Nichol Avenue was to share with De Russey's Lane, in which the bodies were found, the morbid interest of a whole nation four years later, when the case was finally brought to trial. What actually happened in De Russey's Lane on the night of September 14th? What actually happened at 23 Nichol Avenue the same night? For the researcher, it is a matter of an involved and voluminous court record, colorful and exciting in places, confused and repetitious in others. Two things, however, stand out as sharply now as they did on the day of their telling: the pig woman's story of the people she saw in De Russey's Lane that night, and Willie Stevens' story of what went on in the house in Nichol

Avenue. Willie's story, brought out in cross-examination by a prosecutor whose name you may have forgotten (it was Alexander Simpson), lacked all the gaudy melodrama of the pig woman's tale, but in it, and in the way he told it on the stand, was the real drama of the Hall-Mills trial. When the State failed miserably in its confident purpose of breaking Willie Stevens down, the verdict was already written on the wall. The rest of the trial was anticlimax. The jury that acquitted Willie, and his sister, Mrs. Frances Stevens Hall, and his brother, Henry Stevens, was out only five hours.

A detailed recital of all the fantastic events and circumstances of the Hall-Mills case would fill a large volume. If the story is vague in your mind, it is partly because its edges, even under the harsh glare of investigation, remained curiously obscure and fuzzy. Everyone remembers, of course, that the minister was deeply involved with Mrs. Mills, who sang in his choir; their affair had been for some time the gossip of their circle. He was forty-one, she was in her early thirties; Mrs. Hall was past fifty. On the 14th of September, Mr. Hall had dinner at home with his wife, Willie Stevens, and a little niece of Mrs. Hall's. After dinner, he said, according to his wife and his brother-in-law, that he was going to call on Mrs. Mills. There was something about a payment on a doctor's bill. Mrs. Mills had had an operation and the Halls had paid for it (Mrs. Hall had inherited considerable wealth from her parents). He left the house at about the same time, it came out later, that Mrs. Mills left her house, and the two were found murdered, under a crab apple tree in De Russey's Lane, on the edge of town, some forty hours later. Around the bodies were scattered love letters which the choir singer had written to the minister. No weapons were found, but there were several cartridge shells from an automatic pistol.

The investigation that followed – marked, said one New Jersey lawyer, by "bungling stupidity" – resulted in the failure of the Grand Jury to indict anyone. Willie Stevens was questioned for hours, and so was Mrs. Hall. The pig woman told her extraordinary story of what she saw and heard in the lane that night, but she failed to impress the Grand Jurors. Four years went by, and the Hall-Mills case was almost forgotten by people outside of New Brunswick when, in a New Jersey court, one Arthur Riehl brought suit against his wife, the former Louise Geist, for annulment of their marriage. Louise Geist had been, at the time of the murders, a maid in the Hall household. Riehl said in the course of his testimony that his wife had told him "she knew all about the case but had been given $5,000 to hold her tongue." This was all that Mr. Philip Payne, managing editor of the *Daily Mirror*, nosing around for a big scandal of some sort, needed. His newspaper "played up" the story until finally, under its goading, Governor Moore of New Jersey appointed Alexander Simpson special prosecutor with orders to reopen the case. Mrs. Hall and Willie Stevens were arrested and so was their brother, Henry Stevens, and a cousin, Henry de la Bruyere Carpender.

At a preliminary hearing in Somerville the pig woman, with eager stridency, told her story again. About 9 o'clock on the night of September 14th, she heard a wagon going along Hamilton Road near the farm on which she raised her pigs. Thieves had been stealing her corn and she thought maybe they were at it again. So she saddled her mule, Jenny (soon to become the most famous quadruped in the country), and set off in grotesque pursuit. In the glare of an automobile's headlights in De Russey's Lane, she saw a woman with white hair who was wearing a tan coat, and a man with a heavy mustache, who looked like a colored man. These figures she identified as Mrs. Hall and Willie Stevens. Tying her mule to a cedar tree, she started toward the scene on foot and heard voices raised in quarrel: "Somebody said something about letters." She now saw three persons (later on she increased this to four), and a flashlight held by one of them illumined the face of a man she identified first as Henry Carpender, later as Henry Stevens, and it "glittered on something" in the man's hand. Suddenly there was a shot, and as she turned and ran for her mule, there were three more shots; a woman's voice screamed, "Oh, my! Oh, my! Oh, my!" and the voice of another woman moaned, "Oh, Henry!" The pig woman rode wildly home on her mule, without investigating further. But she had lost one of her moccasins in her flight, and some three hours later, at 1 o'clock, she rode her mules back again to see if she could find it. This time, by the light of the moon, she saw Mrs. Hall, she said, kneeling in the lane, weeping. There was no one else there. The pig woman did not see any bodies.

Mrs. Jane Gibson became, because of her remarkable story, the chief witness for the State, as Willie Stevens was to become the chief witness for the defense. If he and his sister were not in De Russey's Lane, as the pig woman had shrilly insisted, it remained for them to tell the detailed story of their whereabouts and their actions that night after Mr. Hall left the house. The Grand Jury this time indicted all four persons implicated by the pig woman, and the trial began on November 3rd, 1926.

The first persons Alexander Simpson called to the stand were "surprise witnesses." They were a Mr. and Mrs. John S. Dixon, who lived in North Plainfield, New Jersey, about twelve miles from New Brunswick. It soon became apparent that they were to form part of a net that Simpson was preparing to draw around Willie Stevens. They testified that at about 8:30 on the night of the murders Willie had appeared at their house, wearing a loose-fitting suit, a derby, a wing collar with bow tie, and, across his vest, a heavy gold chain to which was attached a gold watch. He had said that his sister had let him out there from her automobile and that he was trying to find the Parker Home for the Aged, which was at Bound Brook. He stuttered and he told them that he was an epileptic. They directed him to a trolley car and he went stumbling away. When Mrs. Dixon identified Willie as her visitor, she walked over to him and took his right hand and shook it vigorously, as if to wring recognition out of him. Willie stared at her, said nothing. When she returned to the stand, he grinned widely. That was one of many bizarre incidents which marked the progress of the famous murder trial. It deepened the mystery that hung about the strange figure of Willie Stevens. People could hardly wait for him to take the stand.

William Carpender Stevens had sat in court for sixteen days before he was called to the witness chair, on the 23rd of November, 1926. On that day the trial of Albert B. Fall and Edward L. Doheny, defendants in the notorious Teapot Dome scandal, opened in Washington, but the nation had eyes only for a small, crowded courtroom in Somerville, New Jersey. Willie Stevens, after all these weeks, after all these years, was to speak out in public for the first time. As the New York *Times* said, "He had been pictured as 'Crazy Willie', as a town character, as an oddity, as a butt for all manner of jokes. He had been compared inferentially to an animal, and the hint of an alien racial strain in his parentage had been thrown at him." Moreover, it had been prophesied that Willie would "blow up" on the stand, that he would be trapped into contradictions by the "wily" and "crafty" Alexander Simpson, that he would be tricked finally into blurting out his guilt. No wonder there was no sound in the courtroom except the heavy tread of Willie Stevens' feet as he walked briskly to the witness stand.

Willie Stevens was an ungainly, rather lumpish man, about five feet ten inches tall. Although he looked flabby, this was only because of his loose-fitting clothes and the way he wore them; despite his fifty-four years, he was a man of great physical strength. He had a large head and a face that would be hard to forget. His head was covered with a thatch of thick, bushy hair, and his heavy black eyebrows seemed always to be arched, giving him an expression of perpetual surprise. This expression was strikingly accentuated by large, prominent eyes which, seen through the thick lenses of the spectacles he always wore, seemed to bulge unnaturally. He had a heavy, drooping, walrus mustache, and his complexion was dark. His glare was sudden and fierce; his smile, which came just as quickly, lighted up his whole face and gave him the wide, beaming look of an enormously pleased child. Born in Aiken, South Carolina, Willie Stevens had been brought to New Brunswick when he was two years old. When his wealthy parents died, a comfortable trust fund was left to Willie. The other children, Frances and Henry, had inherited their money directly. Once, when Mrs. Hall was asked if it was not true that Willie was "regarded as essential to be taken care of in certain things", she replied, "In certain aspects". The quality of Willie's mentality, the extent of his eccentricity, were matters the prosecution strove to establish on several occasions. Dr. Laurence Runyon, called by the defense to testify that Willie was not an epileptic and had never stuttered, was cross-examined by Simpson. Said the Doctor, "He may not be absolutely normal mentally, but he is able to take care of himself perfectly well. He is brighter than the average person, although he has never advanced as far in school learning as some others. He reads books that are above the average and makes a good many people look like fools." "A sort of genius, in a way, I suppose?" said Simpson. To which the Doctor quietly replied, "Yes, that is just what I mean."

There were all sorts of stories about Willie. One of them was that he had once started a fire in his back yard and then, putting on a fireman's helmet, had doused it gleefully with a pail of water. It was known that for years he had spent most of every day at the firehouse of Engine Company No. 3 in Dennis Street, New Brunswick. He played cards with the firemen, ran errands for them, argued and joked with them, and was a general favorite. Sometimes he went out and bought a steak, or a chicken, and it was prepared and eaten in the firehouse by the firemen and Willie. In the days when the engine company had been a volunteer organization, Willie was an honorary member and always carried, in the firemen's parades, a flag he had bought and presented to the firehouse, an elaborate banner costing sixty or seventy dollars. He had also bought the black-and-white bunting with which the front of the firehouse was draped whenever a member of the company died.

After his arrest, he had whiled away the time in his cell reading books on metallurgy. There was a story that when his sister-in-law, Mrs. Henry Stevens, once twitted him on his heavy reading, he said, "Oh, that is merely the bread and butter of my literary repast." The night before the trial opened, Willie's chief concern was about a new blue suit that had been ordered for him and that did not fit him to his satisfaction. He had also lost a collar button, and that worried him; Mrs. Henry Stevens hurried to the jail before the court convened and brought him another one, and he was happy. At the preliminary hearing weeks before, Simpson had declared with brutal directness that Willie Stevens did indeed look like a colored man, as the pig woman had said. At this Willie had half risen from his chair and bared his teeth, as if about to leap on the prosecutor. But he had quickly subsided. All through the trial he had sat quietly, staring. He had been enormously interested when the pig woman, attended by a doctor and a nurse, was brought in on a stretcher to give her testimony. This was the man who now, on trial for his life, climbed into the witness chair in the courtroom at Somerville.

There was an immense stir. Justice Charles W. Parker rapped with his gavel. Mrs. Hall's face was strained and white; this was an ordeal she and her family had been dreading for weeks. Willie's left hand gripped his chair tightly, his right hand held a yellow pencil with which he had fiddled all during the trial. He faced the roomful of eyes tensely. His own lawyer, Senator Clarence E. Case, took the witness first. Willie started badly by understating his age ten years. He said he was forty-four. "Isn't it fifty-four?" asked Case. Willie gave the room his great, beaming smile. "Yes," he chortled, boyishly, as if amused by his slip. The spectators smiled. It didn't take Willie long to dispose of the Dixons, the couple who had sworn he stumbled into their house the night of the murder. He answered half a dozen questions on this point with strong emphasis, speaking slowly and clearly: he had never worn a derby, he had never had epilepsy, he had never stuttered, he had never had a gold watch and chain. Mr. Case held up Willie's old silver watch and chain for the jury to see. When he handed them back, Willie, with fine nonchalance, compared his watch with the clock on the courtroom wall, gave his sister a large, reassuring smile, and turned to his questioner with respectful attention. He described, with technical accuracy, an old revolver of his (the murders had been done with an automatic pistol, not a revolver, but a weapon of the same caliber as Willie's). He said he used to fire off the gun on the Fourth of July; remembering these old holidays, his eyes lighted up with childish glee. From this mood he veered suddenly into indignation and anger. "When was the last time you saw the revolver?" was what set him off. "The last time I saw it was in this courthouse!" Willie almost shouted. "I think it was in October, 1922, when I was taken and put through a very severe grilling by – I cannot mention every person's name, but I remember Mr. Toolan, Mr. Lamb, and Detective David, and they did everything but strike me. They cursed me frightfully." The officers had got him into an automobile "by a subterfuge", he charged. "Mr. David said he simply wanted me to go out in the country, to ask me a very few questions, that I would not be very long." It transpired later that on his trip Willie himself had had a question to ask Detective David: would the detective, if they passed De Russey's Lane, be kind enough to point it out to him? Willie had never seen the place, he told the detective, in his life. He said that Mr. David showed him where it was.

When Willie got to the night of September 14th, 1922, in his testimony his anger and indignation were gone; he was placid, attentive, and courteous. He explained quietly that he had come home for supper that night, had gone to his room afterward, and "remained in the house, leaving it at 2:30 in the morning with my sister". Before he went to bed, he said, he had closed his door to confine to his own room the odor of tobacco smoke from his pipe. "Who objected to that?" asked Mr. Case. Willie gave his sudden, beaming grin. "Everybody," he said, and won the first of several general laughs from the courtroom. Then he told the story of what happened at 2:30 in the morning. It is necessary, for a well-rounded picture of Willie Stevens, to give it here at some length. "I was awakened by my sister knocking at my door," said Willie, "and I immediately rose and went to the door and she said, 'I want you to come down to the church, as Edward has not come home; I am very much worried' – or words to that effect. I immediately got dressed and accompanied her down to the church. I went through the front door, followed a small path that led directly to the back of the house past the cellar door. We went directly down Redmond Street to Jones Avenue, from Jones Avenue we went to George Street; turning into George Street we went directly down to Commercial Avenue. There our movements were blocked by an immense big freight automobile. We had to wait there maybe half a minute until it went by, going toward New York.

"I am not at all sure whether we crossed right there at Commercial Avenue or went a little further down George Street and went diagonally across to the church. Then we stopped there and looked at the church to see whether there were any lights. There were no lights burning. Then Mrs. Hall said, 'We might as well go down and see if it could not be possible that he was at the Mills' house.' We went down there, down George Street until we came to Carman Street, turned down Carman Street, and got in front of the Mills' house and stood there two or three minutes to see if there were any lights in the Mills' apartment. There were none." Willie then described, street by street, the return home, and ended with "I opened the front door with my latchkey. If you wish me, I will show it to you. My sister said, 'You might as well go to bed. You can do no more good.' With that I went upstairs to bed." This was the story that Alexander Simpson had to shake. But before Willie was turned over to him, the witness told how he heard that his brother-in-law had been killed. "I remember I was in the parlor," said Willie, "reading a copy of the New York *Times*. I heard someone coming up the steps and I glanced up and I heard my aunt, Mrs. Charles J. Carpender, say, 'Well, you might as well know it – Edward has been shot.' " Willie's voice was thick with emotion. He was asked what happened then. "Well," he said, "I simply let the paper go – that way" (he let his left hand fall slowly and limply to his side) "and I put my head down, and I cried." Mr. Case asked him if he was present at, or had anything to do with, the murder of Mr. Hall and Mrs. Mills. "Absolutely nothing at all!" boomed Willie, coming out of his posture of sorrow, belligerently erect. The attorney for the defense turned, with a confident little bow, to Alexander Simpson. The special prosecutor sauntered over and stood in front of the witness. Willie took in his breath sharply.

Alexander Simpson, a lawyer, a state senator, slight, perky, capable of harsh tongue-lashings, given to sarcasm and innuendo, had intimated that he would "tie Willie Stevens into knots". Word had gone around that he intended to "flay" the eccentric fellow. Hence his manner now came as a surprise. He spoke in a gentle, almost inaudible voice, and his attitude was one of solicitous friendliness. Willie, quite unexpectedly, drew first blood. Simpson asked him if he had ever earned his livelihood. "For about four or five years," said Willie, "I was employed by Mr. Siebold, a contractor." Not having anticipated an affirmative reply, Simpson paused. Willie leaned forward and said, politely, "Do you wish his address?" He did this in good faith, but the spectators took it for what the *Times* called a "sally", because Simpson had been in the habit of letting loose a swarm of investigators on anyone whose name was brought into the case. "No, thank you," muttered Simpson, above a roar of laughter. The prosecutor now set about picking at Willie's story of the night of September 14th: he tried to find out why the witness and his sister had not knocked on the Mills' door to see if Mr. Hall were there. Unfortunately for the steady drumming of questions, Willie soon broke the prosecutor up with another laugh. Simpson had occasion to mention a New Brunswick boarding house called The Bayard, and he pronounced "Bay" as it is spelled. With easy politeness, Willie corrected him. "*Bi*yard," said Willie. "Biyard?" repeated Simpson. Willie smiled, as at an apt pupil. Simpson bowed slightly. The spectators laughed again.

Presently the witness made a slip, and Simpson pounced on it like a stooping falcon. Asked if he had not, at the scene of the murder, stood "in the light of an automobile while a woman on a mule went by", Willie replied, "I never remember that occurrence." Let us take up the court record from there. "Q – You would remember if it occurred, wouldn't you? A. – I certainly would, but I don't remember of ever being in an automobile and the light from the automobile shone on a woman on a mule. Q. – Do you say you were not there, or you don't remember? A. – I say positively I was not there. Q. – Why did you say you don't *remember?* A. – Does not that cover the same thing? Q. – No, it don't, because you might be there and not remember it. A. – Well, I will withdraw that, if I may, and say I was not there positively." Willie assumed an air of judicial authority as he "withdrew" his previous answer, and he spoke his positive denial with sharp decision. Mr. Simpson abruptly tried a new tack. "You have had a great deal of experience in life, Mr. Stevens," he said, "and have read a great deal, they say, and know a lot about human affairs. Don't you think it sounds rather fishy when you say you got up in the middle of the night to go and look for Dr. Hall and went to the house and never even knocked on the door – with your experience of human affairs and people that you met and all that sort of thing – don't that seem rather fishy to you?" There was a loud bickering of attorneys before Willie could say anything to this. Finally Judge Parker turned to the witness and said, "Can you answer that, Mr. Stevens?" "The only way I can answer it, Your Honor," said Willie, scornfully, "is that I don't see that it is at all 'fishy'." The prosecutor jumped to something else: "Dr. Hall's church was not your church, was it?" he asked. "He was not a *Doctor*, sir," said Willie, once more the instructor. "He was the Reverend *Mister* Hall." Simpson paused, nettled. "I am glad you corrected me on that," he said. The courtroom laughed again.

The prosecutor now demanded that Willie repeat his story of what happened at 2:30 A.M. He hoped to establish, he intimated, that the witness had learned it "by rote". Willie calmly went over the whole thing again, in complete detail, but no one of his sentences was the same as it had been. The prosecutor asked him to tell it a third time. The defense objected vehemently. Simpson vehemently objected to the defense's objection. The Court: "We will let him tell it once more." At this point Willie said, "May I say a word?" "Certainly," said Simpson. "Say all you want." Weighing his words carefully, speaking with slow emphasis, Willie said, "All I have to say is I was never taught, as you insinuate, by any person whatsoever. That is my best recollection from the time I started out with my sister to this present minute." Simpson did not insist further on a third recital. He wanted to know now how Willie could establish the truth of his statement that he was in his room from 8 or 9 o'clock until his sister knocked on the door at 2:30 A.M. "Why," said Willie, "if a person sees me go upstairs and does not see me come downstairs, isn't that a conclusion that I was in my room?" The court record shows that Mr. Simpson replied, "Absolutely." "Well," said Willie expansively, "that is all there was to it." Nobody but the pig woman had testified to seeing Willie after he went up to his room that night. Barbara Tough, a servant who had been off during the day, testified that she got back to the Hall home about 10 o'clock and noticed that Willie's door was closed (Willie had testified that it wouldn't stay closed unless he locked it). Louise Geist, of the annulment suit, had testified that she had not seen Willie that night after dinner. It was Willie's story against the pig woman's. That day in court he over-shadowed her. When he stepped down from the witness chair, his shoulders were back and he was smiling broadly. Headlines in the *Times* the next day said, "Willie Stevens Remains Calm Under Cross-Examination. Witness a Great Surprise." There was a touch of admiration, almost of partisanship, in most of the reporters' stories. The final verdict could be read between the lines. The trial dragged on for another ten days, but on the 3rd of December, Willie Stevens was a free man.

He was glad to get home. He stood on the porch of 23 Nichol Avenue, beaming at the house. Reporters had followed him there. He turned to them and said, solemnly, "It is one hundred and four days since I've been here. And I want to get in." They let him go. But two days later, on a Sunday, they came back and Mrs. Hall received them in the drawing room. They could hear Willie in an adjoining room, talking spiritedly. He was, it came out, discussing metallurgy with the Rev. J. Mervin Pettit, who had succeeded Mr. Hall as rector of the Church of St. John the Evangelist.

Willie Stevens, going on seventy, no longer visits the firehouse of No. 3 Engine Company. His old friends have caught only glimpses of him in the past few years, for he has been in feeble health, and spends most of his time in his room, going for a short ride now and then in his chauffeur-driven car. The passerby, glancing casually into the car, would not recognize the famous figure of the middle 1920's. Willie has lost a great deal of weight, and the familiar beaming light no longer comes easily to his eyes.

After Willie had been acquitted and sent home, he tried to pick up the old routine of life where he had left it, but people turned to stare after him in the street, and boys were forever at his heels, shouting, "Look out, Willie, Simpson is after you!" The younger children were fond of him and did not tease him, and once in a while Willie could be seen playing with them, as boisterously and whimsically as ever. The firemen say that if he encountered a ragged child he would find out where it lived, and then give one of his friends the money to buy new clothes for it. But Willie's adventures in the streets of the town became fewer and farther apart. Sometimes months would elapse between his visits to the firehouse. When he did show up in his old haunts, he complained of headaches, and while he was still in his fifties, he spent a month in bed with a heart ailment. After that, he stayed close to home, and the firemen rarely saw him. If you should drop by the firehouse, and your interest in Willie seems friendly, they will tell you some fond stories about him.

One winter Willie took a Cook's tour to Hawaii. When he came back, he told the firemen he had joined an organization which, for five dollars, gave its subscribers a closer view of the volcanoes than the ordinary tourist could get. Willie was crazy about the volcanoes. His trip, however, was spoiled, it came out, because someone recognized and pointed him out as the famous Willie

Stevens of the Hall-Mills case. He had the Cook's agent cancel a month's reservation at a hotel and rearrange his schedule so that he could leave on the next ship. He is infuriated by any reference to the murders or to the trial. Some years ago a newspaper printed a paragraph about a man out West who was "a perfect double for Willie Stevens". Someone in the firehouse showed it to Willie and he tore the paper to shreds in a rage.

Willie still spends a great deal of time reading "heavy books" – on engineering, on entomology, on botany. Those who have seen his famous room at 23 Nichol Avenue – he has a friend in to visit him once in a while – say that it is filled with books. He has no use for detective stories or the Western and adventure magazines his friends the firemen read. When he is not reading scientific tomes, he dips into the classics or what he calls the "worthwhile poets." He used to astound the firemen with his wide range of knowledge. There was the day a salesman of shaving materials dropped in at the enginehouse. Finding that Willie had visited St. Augustine, Florida, he mentioned an old Spanish chapel there. Willie described it and gave its history, replete with dates, and greatly impressed the caller. Another time someone mentioned a certain kind of insect which he said was found in this country. "You mean they used to be," said Willie. "That type of insect has been extinct in this country for forty years." It turned out that it had been, too. On still another occasion Willie fell to discussing flowers with some visitor at the firehouse and reeled off a Latin designation – *crassinae carduaceae*, or something of the sort. Then he turned, grinning, to the listening firemen. "Zinnias to you," he said.

Willie Stevens' income from the trust fund established for him is said to be around forty dollars a week. His expenditures are few, now that he is no longer able to go on long trips. The firemen like especially to tell about the time that Willie went to Wyoming, and attended a rodeo. He told the ticket-seller he wanted to sit in a box and the man gave him a single ticket. Willie explained that he wanted the whole box to himself, and he planked down a ten-dollar bill for it. Then he went in and sat in the box all alone. "I had a hell of a time!" he told the firemen gleefully when he came back home.

De Russey's Lane, which Detective David once pointed out to Willie Stevens, is now, you may have heard, entirely changed. Several years ago it was renamed Franklin Boulevard, and where the Rev. Mr. Edward W. Hall and Mrs. Eleanor Mills lay murdered there is now a row of neat brick and stucco houses. The famous crab apple tree under which the bodies were found disappeared the first weekend after the murders. It was hacked to pieces, roots and all, by souvenir-hunters.

21

HELPFUL HINTS AND THE HOVEYS

No sooner have I turned my back, a laborious and rather painful procedure for me nowadays, than some bright-eyed woman or other rises briskly from her escritoire with a brand-new list of nine or ten ways of preventing something or bringing something to pass. In a recent Sunday *Times*, Dr. Josephine Rathbone sets forth ten tricks (she calls them) which will help you to relax and go to sleep. Trick Number One goes like this:

Cut down on the intensity of your thinking half an hour before retiring. (Play Chinese checkers, plan an excursion for the weekend, write a letter to a friend, think of pleasant things you have been doing.)

I lay awake for several hours one night pondering that suggestion. As I tossed and turned, I figured the effect that Trick No. 1 must have had on George Hovey, a nervous, middle-aged insomniac I know. I am sure George saw Dr. Rathbone's list – he never misses anything in the Sunday *Times*. I could see George and his wife Irma sitting in their living room at ten-thirty on the evening of the Sunday Dr. Rathbone's list of tricks appeared . . .

IRMA (*looking up from her mystery novel*): What are you doing now?

GEORGE (*who has not moved or said a word for ten minutes*): Hm? Oh. I am cutting down on the intensity of my thoughts.

IRMA: Well, do you have to look that way?

GEORGE: What way?

IRMA: As if you were crouching to spring.

GEORGE (*angrily, the intensity of his thoughts going way up*): Even if we had some Chinese checkers and I knew how to play, and so did you, I wouldn't play with you.

IRMA: I didn't say anything about playing any Chinese checkers. I –

GEORGE: Let it go, will you – I mean for the God sake!

IRMA: Now, don't start swearing at me. I can't say anything to you any more but what you flare up.

GEORGE: Shut up.

IRMA: You shut up.

GEORGE: You shut up, too.

IRMA: Shut up.

(*Irma goes back to her book, and George closes his eyes and tries to relax. Ten minutes go by.*)

IRMA: You're tightening up again. I can feel it.

GEORGE: I can't think of anything pleasant that's happened to me recently.

IRMA: Well, who can?

GEORGE: I'll either have to write to a friend or plan a weekend excursion.

IRMA: Don't be nasty. I don't care if you do. You haven't got any friends.

GEORGE: Is that so? All yours are ones you met through me.

IRMA: That's such a lie I won't even answer it. Are you trying to make me mad?

GEORGE (*shouting*): You said I didn't have any friends!

IRMA (*yelling*): I mean to write letters to! All your friends are in town. You see them every day.

GEORGE: I don't have to *send* the letter, do I?

(*Irma coldly refuses to answer this idiotic question and goes back to her book. Two minutes pass.*)

IRMA: Where do you think you're going, if I may ask?

GEORGE: Hm? I'm not going anywhere, except to bed – if you will let me cut down on the intensity of my thoughts.

IRMA: You have to stay in town every weekend and work.

GEORGE: I know that. Do you have to rub it in?

IRMA: You said you were going on a weekend excursion.

GEORGE: I said I was *planning* one.

IRMA (*yelling*): If you are planning a weekend excursion, you are going somewhere!

GEORGE (*rising and pacing the floor*): I am not. It's the way Josephine Rathbone gets to sleep.

IRMA: Oh, it is? Well, that's very interesting, I'm sure. And who is Josephine Radburn?

GEORGE: I never heard of her.

You can keep this going as long as you want to, but George has already fallen (or been pushed) into such a state that there will be no sleep for him this night. If you are interested in the good doctor's eight other rules, I'm afraid you'll have to look them up in the Sunday *Times*. The only one that may be said to have fascinated me is No.7, which suggests that you go to bed "a little damp and chilly" from your bath. So much for Dr. Rathbone.

Now we come to Helen Haberman and her list of nine ways to keep calm and thus avoid stomach disorders. This list was included in an article by Mrs. Haberman which appeared in a recent issue of *Cosmopolitan*. Let us, before we print the nine helpful hints, look in on the Hoveys again. It is a little past midnight and Irma sits in the living room glaring at George. The Hoveys have had six guests for dinner, all of whom have just left . . .

IRMA: Well, you certainly made a spectacle of *yourself* tonight.

GEORGE: What did I do?

IRMA: What didn't you do? First you were dull, and you talked in such a low voice nobody could understand you. You just sat there, like a bump on a log. Then you *did* everything so badly. You hacked up the roast, you slopped up the drinks – and you thought it was funny. Anyway, you tried to get people to laugh at you.

GEORGE: Go on. That can't be *all* I did.

IRMA: Well, I should say it wasn't. You missed the point of all the stories everybody told – you acted as if you were listening with only one ear to what was being said. I don't know what they thought of you, but I'm sure they'll never come here again – any of them.

GEORGE: What else did I do, pet?

IRMA: Don't call me pet! You were so selfish. You emptied your own ash-tray from time to time, but you wouldn't empty old Dr. Townsend's, although it was right on the table next to you. George, I've never heard of any man acting like you did tonight. It was disgraceful. I was never so humiliated in my life.

GEORGE: Are you finished now?

IRMA: I am not. You were as disagreeable as you could be to all the girls. "No!" you kept saying, no matter what they asked you. And you ended up growling and grumbling. What's got into you, anyway, for the God sake?

GEORGE: I *got* to act that way.

IRMA: What do you mean, you got to act that way?

GEORGE: I got to do it to avoid stomach disorders. Here, read this. (*He hands her Mrs. Haberman's list of nine ways of avoiding worry and its resulting ailments.*)

In case you, too, were puzzled by George's behavior, as described by Mrs. Hovey, here are the helpful hints for a peaceful mind and a happy stomach, which George was dutifully following out:

Be a little dull. A low voice and quiet manner may make you seem dull to some people, but risk it for the sake of harmony and ease.

Do things badly. There's no harm in falling short of perfection the first time you try something new. The important thing is to want to do something ardently enough to risk doing it at all.

Let people laugh at you. Keep your own sense of humor active, and it won't matter whether people laugh *at* you or *with* you.

Be disagreeable. Say no often. Develop your own interests and stick to them stubbornly.

Cultivate laziness. If you're a natural worrier, it goes without saying that you rush and bustle. Slow down.

Miss the point occasionally. Don't always strain to get the other fellow's views. Don't always try to argue back. Deliberately listen with only one ear now and then.

Practice selfishness. Do your own work first. Don't let others monopolize you.

Be a bump on a log. It takes plenty of stolid sitting to withstand times of national stress like these. You needn't apologize for inaction.

Growl and grumble. Don't keep your feelings bottled up. There's nothing like a good healthy "mad" to relieve strained feelings.

Mrs. Haberman, in her article, gives several case histories. The one that interests me most is as follows:

Case B: An attractive young married woman has a stomach attack every day. "Does it occur at any particular hour?" the doctor asks. "Yes, every night at dinner." It develops that her mother-in-law, who lives with them, eats lunch in her room but joins the family for dinner. "Tell your husband to have his mother eat upstairs," the doctor advises. She makes the suggestion tactfully, the change is arranged, and her stomach doesn't bother her again.

Let us see how the good doctor's advice would work out in actual practice. I take you again to the home of George Hovey, whose mother has been living with him and Irma for some months now. It is 5 P.M. and the Hoveys are alone in their living room, old Mrs. Hovey not having returned from a trip to the Sixth Avenue shooting galleries . . .

IRMA: Sometimes I think your mother has the pleasantest room in the house. It would make a very cheerful dining room.

GEORGE: Hm?

IRMA: I often go in there to eat when I'm here alone. I think a person eats more in a cheerful room like that.

GEORGE: What are you talking about, Irma?

IRMA: I was just thinking that your mother would be happier if she ate dinner in her room.

GEORGE: She eats her lunch there now and I can't see that that makes her very happy. What does she eat her lunch in there for, anyway?

IRMA: Oh, she really loves eating in there, George.

GEORGE: And you say you'd rather eat there than in any room in the house. Well, eat your lunch in there with Mamma if you want to, I don't care.

IRMA (*clutching at her stomach*): You don't see what I mean, George. It's for your mother's sake, really. She eats so little at dinner that it – well, it gives me stomach trouble. Then that worries *her*.

GEORGE: I don't see how it could. Mamma was telling me the other day that you have stomach trouble because you stuff yourself.

IRMA: Indeed!

GEORGE: How could her eating so little affect *your* stomach, for the God sake?

IRMA (*yelling*): Everything she does affects my stomach!

I can't bear the sight of her sitting there! She eats as if she were chewing dice. She –

GEORGE: Is that so! At least she is a lady and she went to school, which is more than you can say about your mother.

And so it goes. Each time I try to write a scene in which Irma tactfully gets George to make Mamma eat dinner in her room, the Hoveys end up screaming and blaspheming. Perhaps one of you ladies will sit down and write out a list of nine or ten ways of persuading a husband to keep his mother out of the dining room. It's too much for me.

22

MEMORIAL

She came all the way from Illinois by train in a big wooden crate 13 years ago, a frightened black poodle, not yet a year old. She felt terrible in body and worse in mind. These contraptions that men put on wheels, in contravention of that law of nature which holds that the feet must come in contact with the ground in travelling, dismayed her. She was never able to ride 1000 yards in an automobile without getting sick at her stomach, but she was always apologetic about this frailty, never, as she might well have been, reproachful.

She tried patiently at all times to understand Man's way of life: the rolling of his wheels, the raising of his voice, the ringing of his bells; the way of searching out with lights the dark protecting corners of the night; his habit of building his beds inside walls, high above the nurturing earth. She refused, with all courtesy, to accept his silly notion that it is better to bear puppies in a place made of machined wood and clean blue cloth than in the dark and warm dirt beneath the oak flooring of the barn.

The poodle was hand in glove with natural phenomena. She raised two litters of puppies, 11 each time, taking them in her stride, the way she took the lightning and the snow. One of these litters, which arrived ahead of schedule, was discovered under the barn floor by a little girl of four. The child gaily displayed on her right forearm the almost invisible and entirely painless marks of teeth which had gently induced her to put down the live black toys she had found and wanted to play with.

The poodle had no vices that I can think of, unless you could count her incurable appetite for the tender tips of the young asparagus in the garden and for the black raspberries when they ripened on the bushes in the orchard. Sometimes, as punishment for her depredations, she walked into bees' nests or got her long shaggy ears tangled in fence wire. She never snarled about the penalties of existence or whimpered about the trials and grotesqueries of life with Man.

She accepted gracefully the indignities of the clipping machine which, in her maiden days, periodically made a clown of her for the dog shows, in accordance with the stupid and unimaginative notion, inherited from the drunken Romans, that this most sensitive and dignified of animals is at heart a fool. The poodle, which can look as husky as a Briard when left shaggy, is an outdoors dog and can hold its own in the field with the best of the retrievers, including the Labrador.

The poodle won a great many ribbons in her bench days, and once went best of breed at Madison Square

Garden, but she would have traded all her medals for a dish of asparagus. She knew it was show time when a red rubber bib was tied around her neck. That meant a ride in a car. I used to ride with her in the rumble seat, and once, on our way to Newport, when the rain came down suddenly, there was I with one hand on the poodle's shoulder and the other holding over her a bright green parasol. The highways of New England have, I am sure, seldom beheld a more remarkable sight.

Like the great Gammeyer of Tarkington's *Gentle Julia*, the poodle I knew seemed sometimes about to bridge the mysterious and conceivably narrow gap that separates instinct from reason. She could take part in your gaiety and your sorrow; she trembled to your uncertainties and lifted her head at your assurances. There were times when she seemed to come close to a pitying comprehension of the whole troubled scene and what lies ticking behind it. If poodles, who walk so easily upon their hind legs, ever do learn the little tricks of speech and reason, I should not be surprised if they made a better job of it than Man, who would seem to be slowly slipping back to all fours, in spite of Van Wyck Brooks and Lewis Mumford and Robert Frost.

The poodle kept her sight, her hearing, and her figure up to her quiet and dignified end. She knew that the Hand was upon her and she accepted it with a grave and unapprehensive resignation. This, her dark intelligent eyes seemed to be trying to tell me, is simply the closing of full circle, this is the flower that grows out of Beginning; this – not to make it too hard for you, friend – is as natural as eating the raspberries and raising the puppies and riding into the rain.

Part Two

FOREWORD

The stories that follow were written in Europe, most of them in France, in 1937 and 1938, so far away, so long ago. Since France, whenever I was there, made my heart a lighted place, these small, random essays are neither searching nor troubled. Everyone in those ending years of an epoch must have had some sense of the dreadful shadow ahead, there were so many signs and intimations. I left the examination and report of all this to those better equipped for such a task, and set out to drive the long, straight, quiet roads of France, and to walk the old familiar streets of favorite towns. These are merely pieces of the color and pattern of the surface which is to me the loveliest in the world. Anything written about France out of lightness of heart must seem now a little melancholy and incongruous. My hope in reprinting these stories is that they may start up some bright, cherished memory of the France which so many of us will always love, the France which we know will rise again.

1

YOU KNOW HOW THE FRENCH ARE

It is touch and go (*il s'en faut de bien peu*) which is harder for an American in Europe to understand: the report of a cricket match in the *Daily Mail* or an account, anywhere, of what is going on in French political circles. On my two previous visits to France I never came close to understanding what was going on in French political circles (cricket I gave up long ago), so this time, before I sailed, I decided to buy some helpful books on the subject to read on the voyage over. I got Alexander Werth's "Which Way France?" (in spite of a title that sounded as if Mr. Werth wasn't very sure of what was going on himself); Mr. Gunther's "Inside Europe," which has several chapters on France; and a book on government by M. Léon Blum, written in French. This last, since I couldn't get anything out of it, I gave to a French steward on the *Ile-de France* who turned out to be a Royalist and after that would not answer the bell when I rang for him.

Everybody in Paris, from messenger boys on up and

down, is very politically minded and know lots more than you and I do, or at any rate can talk much faster. I noticed the other day in the Parc Monceau, that loveliest of all green places, a small boy and girl playing Gaston Calmette and Mme. Caillaux, the principal figures in the notorious French political shooting of almost twenty-five years ago. All the little children in Paris play with toy pistols, but they don't play cops and robbers, they play editors and politicians. Now and again a frowning tot of five or six will toddle to a wall and with a piece of chalk mark on it *"Vive Maurras!"* or *"Les Soviets partout!"* or *"A bas les deux ans!"* or some other slogan of a timely political nature. It is somehow grimmer than the childish gangster hunts in our own parks and corner lots.

It is essential to know the names of a few French politicians when you are in France, if only to hold your own in the repartee and invective of the street. For example, if you refuse money to a French beggar, he is sure to shout after you that you are undoubtedly a member of whatever political party he suspects is trying to deliver France into the hands of her enemies. (All the political parties are trying to do that, I find in reading the various Paris papers.) In such a case all you have to do is shout back at your heckler the names of whatever politicians spring to mind: "Laval! Daladier! Flandin! Chéron!" Since all French party leaders are unpopular, even with their own followers, the names of any of them will serve very handily as epithets and are much stronger than pig, dog, cow, kind of sausage, name of a name, etc. If you are able to bandy the nicknames of the various politicians, so much the better. These nicknames form an important phase of public life in the French Republic and deserve a paragraph of their own.

Almost every one of the thirty daily papers in Paris has an editorial writer or two famous for thinking up nicknames for French politicians. Ridicule has for centuries been the strongest weapon of political assault in France (leading virulence by about half a head) and many a man has been ruined, I am told, by an adroitly bitter nickname, applied to him by some journalist or political opponent at the proper moment in his career. Once in a while the people as a whole apply the nickname (France is a race of wags), in which case the *malheureux* (the poor sap) is likely to be laughed out of public life in no time. Even if he survives, his dignity and importance are forever lessened. Take the case of M. Albert Lebrun. Shortly after he took office as President of France, he posed for the sound reels with his family, which included a tiny grandchild that began to cry as the cameras ground – and the sound apparatus recorded. M. Lebrun bounced the infant up and down on his knee, saying over and over again, for all France to hear, "Pooh, pooh – pooh, pooh" ("pooh" in French is "*pouh*", but it's pronounced the same way). M. Lebrun has been known from that day, from one corner of the Republic to the other, as "Pooh Pooh". This name will stick to him forever. If he should ever form a cabinet, it would probably be pooh-poohed out of existence. What a day it would have been for France when Al Smith called Franklin Roosevelt "old potato" that time, had the two men been French politicians instead of American! The minor pleasantry was lost sight of in America in a few weeks, but a French political figure who had been called "old potato" would have gone to his grave as "*la vieille pomme de terre*".

It strikes me as a little diappointing that in a country which devotes itself to thinking up nicknames for politicians as Americans think up nicknames for athletes, there should be so little ingenuity, sharpness, and wit in the invention of them. There is, for example, the case of M. Albert Sarraut, a former Premier. In his late sixties, M. Sarraut, according to Mr. Werth, looks "sometimes like a village *curé*, and sometimes like Mr. Pickwick, with an unfortunate platform manner, and a verbose, florid style of oratory". You would think the boys would have gouged something pretty funny out of that, but M. Sarraut is known simply as *le Sphinx*, after a night club of that name in Montparnasse which he is fond of attending. This was good for a big laugh, however, when he was Premier, and is still good for a big laugh. M. Laval is known, uproariously, as *Le Bougnat*, which means both "a resident of Auvergne" and "coal-and-wood man" (I understand you have to be French to see the subtle humor of this). Camille Chautemps was long ago damned with the name "*Le Ténébreux*", which means "the Shadowy One"; André Tardieu suffers frightfully under all the dire implications of "The Shark"; and some genius of the boulevards or the *couloirs* thought of calling M. Flandin, who is six feet four inches tall, *Le Gratte-Ciel* (the Skyscraper). At a meeting he addressed one time, Colonel de La Rocque, the Croix de Feu leader, referred to the portly

M. Herriot as "The Fat One" and brought down the house. And so it goes, one laugh after another.

This brings us to the actual workings of the French government, to what goes on in the Chamber of Deputies. The Chamber, as everyone knows, is divided into the Left, the Center, and the Right. If you think that you are now about to grasp the nature and composition of the famous French legislative body, you are crazy. Mr. Werth himself, who has for years studied the Chamber of Deputies as correspondent for the Manchester *Guardian*, has to go into some pretty strange and involved footnotes on this subject in his book. One of them is to this effect: Most of the Left Republicans in the Chamber of Deputies do not belong to the Left but to the Center, and are not really Left Republicans at all but members of the *Alliance Democratique* party. Many of the Popular Democrats, who belong to the Right, are really left – or at any rate more Left than the Left Republicans, who belong to the Center. I have quoted Mr. Werth almost exactly – he made it just a little harder to follow than I have.

We must also turn to the invaluable Mr. Werth for an engrossing picture of a French government in action. He tells, on page 207, about a vote of confidence that Laval got in December, 1935, a very, very close vote of confidence, so close that I, for one (and Mr. Werth for another), could hardly call it confidence. It seems that during his speech, before the voting began, M. Laval (*Le Bougnat*) was cheered by both the Right and the Left. "Neither the Right nor the Left believed in Laval's sincerity," Mr. Werth adds, just to mix me up. Now, M.

Laval's speech was a strongly pro-League speech, such a pro-League speech as had not been heard before – "a perfect League speech", Mr. Werth calls it. You can imagine Mr. Werth's surprise, then (and M. Laval's and the League's and mine), when everybody who believed in what M. Laval was saying voted *against* him and all the anti-League men voted *for* him. Says Mr. Werth, "Those who should have been revolted by his speech, voted most readily for Laval. Those who should have been deeply impressed by it, refused him their confidence." At this point in his book, Mr. Werth begins, naturally enough, to ask his readers what the hell happened. "How, indeed," he writes, "did Laval get a majority at all? – for the majority of the house was unquestionably hostile to him." If Mr. Werth, who was there, doesn't know, I'm sure I don't. He sets down, however, five possible reasons for Laval's majority, which was twenty votes, and the last two reasons are rather interesting. It seems that six deputies who voted against Laval were counted as voting for him. Furthermore, there is a drawer or a shelf or something in the Chamber of Deputies which, Mr. Werth says, is known as the *armoire à confiture*, or "jam cupboard". In this drawer (or on this shelf) are kept the blank ballot papers of "half a dozen chronic absentees" (there are always six or eight deputies who never attend the sittings of the Chamber at all, on the ground that there are so many more interesting places to go in Paris). Well, it turns out that in a great emergency, the government can get these ballots and cast them for the government. This is an old, old French custom and persists even though the deputies who stay away and whose votes are cast for the government stay away because they are mad at the government.

In closing, let me tell the story of one French politician who was driven crazy by it all ("became suddenly foolish", as the French say). This was M. Paul Deschanel, who was elected President shortly after the war. Clemenceau had expected to be elected, and when they picked Deschanel, a man whom Mr. Werth describes as colorless, Clemenceau retired to private life, very sore at everybody. But he was to have his revenge. M. Deschanel had not been in the Elysée Palace two days before he began climbing the trees and bathing in the fountain. He was finally made to retire on account of "ill health", although he was having the time of his life. Old Clemenceau, hearing of the bizarre goings-on, got off one of those famous French political quips. "*Alors*," he said, "they thought they were going to get an idiot in me, and they got an idiot anyway." *C'était une fine mouche, le vieux Tigre!* (He was a sly dog, the old Tiger!) It is interesting to note that *mouche*, in the sense used here, means dog, although it ordinarily means fly. It also has some other meanings, which I thought might interest you: it means speck, beauty spot, a short imperial beard, the button of a foil, the bull's-eye of a target, a river passenger steamer, an advice boat, a spy, a parasite, a dun, an unfortunate person, impatience, anger, and a game of cards also known as loo. No wonder the French get mixed up.

2

LA FLEUR DES GUIDES FRANÇAIS

If you are going to drive a car around France you have to have a *Guide Michelin*. Even if you are going to ride on trains or walk you ought to have a *Guide Michelin*, but if you are going to drive you really have to have one. This marvellous volume, of more than a thousand compact pages, has been coming out every year since 1905. When it was thirty years old it was completely reviewed in these pages, but I think it ought to be noticed every three years anyway, for the benefit of those thousands of people just coming of tourist age, some of whom are quite nice. It costs twenty-five francs, which is cheap enough for a priceless book. You can buy one at almost any bookstore or news-stand in France; I got mine in the ship shed at Le Havre last summer. Without it I would be lost. (This is as good a place as any to say that I am not lost without a Baedeker. I also get along perfectly without those "Fly Away with Me!" travel books your niece wrote and the "France" volume of my own aunt's "Here We Go Again!"

series.)

The *Guide Michelin* leads you with a wise and experienced hand into every big city and sizable town and into hundreds of hamlets of the Republic. Its greatest service is this: it tells you where the best hotels and restaurants are and what each chef and *sommelier* prides himself on. There are half a hundred other facts. You can find out at a glance what sights are worth seeing, when the local fairs and carnivals take place, whether there is golf or tennis, what it costs to put your car in a garage, and where you can park and where you can't. Much of *Michelin's* information is conveyed by means of printed symbols the size of a pinhead: a tiny man in a rocking chair, placed after the name of a hotel, means it is located in a quiet quarter; a tiny candle in a holder means there is no electricity. There are excellent maps, too, and these have their own *signes conventionnels*, so that you can tell instantly where the cathedrals, the ruins, the post offices, the grade crossings, and the streetcar lines are, and whether there is a theater, a hospital, a street lined with trees, a wonderful view, or a seaplane base. Let us take the town of Dijon, for example, and see what *Michelin* has to tell us about it.

Dijon, we learn, is in the Côte-d'Or, has a population of 86,544, and if you want to park your car longer than fifteen minutes you have to put it in a parking lot. The city is renowned for its Gastronomical Fair, held every year from October 30th to November 14th. There is no parking at all on the Rue de la Liberté as far up as the Brasserie du Miroir; traffic is prohibited in certain sections of the Street

of the Twenty-sixth Dragoons on market day, Friday.
The places to see are the museum, the Palais des Beaux-
Arts, the old palace of the Dukes of Burgundy, etc. After
this comes a list of the automobile agencies of the town,
where you can go for repairs and accessories: Hispano,
Unic, Talbot, Lancia, Hotchkiss, Licorne, Voisin, Peu-
geot, Delage, Berliet, Panhard, Buick, and Chevrolet.

The section on restaurants is the most interesting,
because Dijon is the headquarters of the gourmets of
France and the gateway to the Burgundy wine country.
It's hard to make up your mind where to eat in Dijon. M.
Racouchot's Aux Trois Faisans invites you with *"Suprème
de brochet dijonnaise, Coq au Chambertin, Poire glacée belle
dijonnaise. Vins: Gevrey-Chambertin Combe au Moine
1929, Meursault Charmes 1933"*. M. Maillard's Grande
Taverne offers *"Jambon du Morvan à la lie de bourgogne,
Escargots au Meursault (création Terminus), Coq au Chambertin. Vins: Chambolle-Musigny, Romanée-Conti"*. We
picked from *Michelin's* list the night we were in Dijon M.
Bony's Au Châteaubriant: *"Châteaubriant, Meurette
d'anguille, Poulet au Chambertin. Vins: Vosne-Romanée
1928, Hospices de Beaune 1919."* You can come out of any
of these restaurants, filled with fine food and glowing with
great wine, for about a dollar and a half per person. To Mr.
Ford Madox Ford, whose long, rambling essay called
"Provence" you would do well to take with you to
southern France when you go, only the small restaurants
are worth while, the ones that require "a little erudition
and a knowledge of back streets" to find. I feel he would
regard many of *Michelin's* selections as what he calls

"gilded palaces" (which none of them really are). Among those who have lived in France for many years it is high heresy to think in terms of dollars. One either pays from five to twenty francs for a meal, which is decent and proper, or from twenty to sixty, which is unholy. I have had some wonderful unholy meals in France for a dollar and a half or two dollars – I will always, I am afraid, think of francs in terms of dollars when it comes to eating.

The rise and fall of the franc, I might put in right here, causes a certain havoc and confusion among some of the guide-books. There is a pamphlet, for instance, called *Les Hôtels de Tourisme en France*, published by a government organization known as Centre National d'Expansion de Tourisme du Thermalisme et du Climatisme (all of that). I have the 1937 edition, but I never use it. It gives a list of French hotels and the prices they charge for rooms. An explanatory note in English says that "The owners and managers of these hotels pledged themselves, during the month of October, 1936, to adhere strictly to the rates published in the official Hotel Guide." That is, to adhere to these rates during 1937, since the book is dated with a big 1937 on the cover, which bears in large type the words *"Prix Garantis"*. Surely ninety per cent of these hotels nevertheless raised their rates after May on account of the depreciation of the franc. One of them, where I stayed in Paris, pledged in this guide that its maximum rate for a room for two persons would be fifty francs a day, but I paid ninety francs for such a room there in September. When I showed the manager of this hotel the official Hotel Guide and the pledge, and his rates, he smiled pleasantly and said to pay no attention to that book – it was just the official government Hotel Guide, full of rates and pledges, signifying nothing. Let us go back again to *Michelin*, which pledges you no pledges.

If you were going to use the *Michelin* guide only for its list of Paris restaurants (about a hundred and twenty, not counting hotel dining rooms), it would be worth the price. The editors use from one to three stars in grading restaurants as to merit of cooking. Six Paris restaurants, it might interest you to know, get three stars *** ("*Une des meilleures tables de France: vaut le voyage. La Fleur de la cuisine française*"). These six are Larue, Tour d'Argent, Lapérouse, Café de Paris, Lucas-Carton, and Foyot's (which closed its doors forever in October). This starring system, by the way, is also used for the antiquities of the various towns, or for what *Michelin* calls "*intérêt des curiosités*". Thus three stars mean that an antiquity is "*très vivement recommandée*"; two stars, "*recommandée*"; one star, "*Intéressante*". If a place is merely listed, without any stars, it should really be seen anyway, the preface says. As an example of the loving care and careful detail with which the guide is got up, you are informed whether a given place of interest outside a town's limits can be reached by car, and if it can't, approximately how long it will take you to get out to it and back on foot. "This does not include," the preface thoughtfully adds, "the time of visiting or appreciating the places of interest."

Truly a wonderful, a monumental book, the *Guide Michelin*. It is got out by the Michelin tire people, and of course it advertises Michelin tires as it goes along, but how gaily and unobtrusively! If you have heard the accusation that there are only two French newspapers in all Paris (*L'Humanité* and *L'Action Française*) in which you cannot buy news space and hence are inclined cynically to believe that perhaps hotelkeepers and restaurateurs can buy stars in *Michelin*, the guide has this proudly to say, "We cannot repeat too often that the independence of the *Guide Michelin* is absolute, that no *hôtelier* can have his place mentioned in this book by any payment of any kind whatsoever or by any kind of favor, direct or indirect." France, in the *Michelin*, has reached a high point in the art of the guidebook.

I have done, I fear, but indifferent justice to the most valuable book in my travelling library, but I must get on to another, the *Guide Gastronomique International*, which concerns itself not at all with the problems of the motorist and has no room for *curiosités*, but deals only with hotels and restaurants, food and wine. Let us first glance for a moment, however, at that enormous volume called "Europa Touring", a motoring guide to Europe published by the American Automobile Association and affiliated clubs. If you bring your car to Europe as a member of the A.A.A. you're sure to get one before you leave New York. It gives information about roads, passports, hotels, restaurants, customs, etc., for all the countries of Europe, in French, English, and German; it is crammed with maps, advertisements, and whatnot. I found the thing formidable to the point of being overwhelming and I put it at the back of the trunk with my skiing things. In France you don't need it; the *Michelin* takes up one-fourth the space and tells you four times as much.

The *Guide Gastronomique International* runs to more than seven hundred pages and is divided into four sections: France; Paris; the French Colonies, Protectorates, and Mandates; and Foreign Countries. The foreign section begins with Albania and ends with New Zealand, touching mysteriously on the United States as it goes along, and dealing in varying detail with the Dutch West Indies, Peru, Germany, India, England, Manchukuo, Palestine, Poland, Siam, Persia, Ceylon, and practically every other place you ever heard of. Lacking the fine accuracy and the calm judgment of the *Michelin*, floundering a bit, stopping now and again for an anecdote, it is nevertheless a fascinating book, interesting to compare with the other guide as you go through France. It lists some two hundred and fifty places to eat in Paris and has a four- instead of a three-star system for restaurants. Of the Paris restaurants that win *Michelin's* highest award only four get *Gastronomique's* blue ribbon: Larue, Tour d'Argent, Lapérouse, and the lamented Foyot. But *Gastronomique* believes that the *fleur* of the *cuisine française* may also be found at L'Escargot, 38 Rue Montorgueil; Prunier (cheers from the American tourists); and a place listed as "Restaurant Candre", 41 Rue St. André-des-Arts. This last is listed by *Michelin* as "Chez Vincent, 1 Rue Eperon" (one star). It is actually located on the corner of the two streets and the only name on the place when we found it was "Maurice Allard", or so I and the lady who travels with me are prepared to swear. But that is another story and, as you see, a pretty confusing one. It is a tiny place and was so crowded we couldn't get in.

Far and away the most interesting part of the *Guide Gastronomique* (I have a 1936 edition, never having been able to find a more recent one) is its section on the United States. This starts, amazingly enough, with Bakersfield, California, and ends with Wilmington, Delaware. Exactly thirty other places are mentioned in between: Beverly Hills, Boston, Briarcliff, Burlington, Cheyenne (you should eat at the Plains Hotel there), Chicago, Denver, Detroit, Fort Worth, Gloucester, Grand Canyon, Hollywood, La Jolla, Lynbrook, L. I., Los Angeles, Newport, Me., New York, New Orleans, Palos Verdes, Pasadena, Paso (El), Portland, Ore., Riverside (I don't know what state, but the Mission Inn is recommended), San Antonio, Santa Barbara, San Diego, San Francisco, Seattle, Washington, D.C., and Wichita.

Fourteen eating places are mentioned in San Francisco, one of them, the White House Hotel, rating one star for food. In Los Angeles, where fifteen places are listed, one star each goes to the Restaurant Alvers, Al Levy's Tavern, and the Mona Lisa Restaurant (I leave the soundness of these judgments to whoever may be interested). In Chicago, *Gastronomique* feels, only two places are worth mentioning: the Blackstone and the Drake. The Blackstone, we are told, "is not modern but is very pleasant and incontestably the *plus chic* place in the city". For the convenience of the traveller, most of the towns and cities are located, in that wild, free manner which is in the very best French tradition. Thus Chicago is "100 miles south of Milwaukee, 275 miles west of Detroit, 300 miles northeast of St. Louis". Washington is "225 miles northwest of New York, 200 miles southeast of Pittsburgh, 600 miles northeast of Atlanta". New York (in case the French voyager leaves his ship at Quarantine and gets lost) is "200 miles southwest of Boston and 225 miles northeast of Washington". Lynbrook is simply "opposite New York" – anyone could find Lynbrook. Seattle and New Orleans are not located – too difficult; it would just be confusing.

La cuisine of New York naturally comes in for the most comprehensive appraisal. Fifty restaurants and hotel dining rooms are mentioned in this great city 225 miles northeast of that very Washington which is 225 miles to the northwest. No place gets four stars or even three, but eight get two stars: the Caviar, Crillon, Cyrano, Madison Hotel, Marguery, Passy ("28 East 63th Street"), Plaza Hotel, and Voisin. Those, to *Gastronomique*, are the great places, *les meilleures tables de New York*, rating two stars more than Childs, which is merely listed, and two fewer than Larue, Tour d'Argent, etc., in Paris. I hope this straightens everything out for you.

There are a number of interesting honorable mentions (no stars), among them the Hotel Blackstone, which, the traveller is assured, will be found at the corner of Fiftieth Street and Fifty-eighth Street, France's Tavern, *Près de Wall Street Downtown* (and named, apparently, after that great Republic 58 miles east of London and 378 miles northwest of Portugal), and Horse Grill, for which no address is given but which I have figured out must mean the old White Horse Tavern. Its excellent steaks and few well-chosen bottles are mentioned. There may be a Horse

Grill in New York for all I know, but if so, I've never been in it. "*Jack et Charlie, 21 W. 52nd, appelé aussi 'Iron Gate*'," does not rate a star, either, but *Gastronomique's* spy reports that this place was "*le meilleur speak-easy de New York au temps de la prohibition. On y trouve toujours d'excellents vins, des liqueurs parfaits et des repas délicieux*". No star, though. The Algonquin is not listed at all, but the Prince George is, and also Moneta's, which is in "Mulbeary Street", and "Richmann-Club", which one learns is an *endroit charmant* with a *décor sympathique*. This lovely haunt of charm and sympathy unhappily no longer exists.

I said somewhere that *Gastronomique* occasionally tells an anecdote, and I suppose I ought to quote one of them. Well, at the Hôtel de l'Europe et Angleterre, in the town of Mâcon, the guide says, the *patron* will never serve more than fifty meals, noon or night, because he doesn't believe a great cook, a *maître queux*, can properly take care of a larger number. It seems that one day an American tourist showed up in the restaurant of the hotel after the fifty had been served and was told that he couldn't eat there – not until dinner time, anyway. In the course of the argument that followed, the American, who was pretty sure he knew how to make arrogant French *patrons* and *chefs* come to time, offered one hundred dollars for his lunch (*vin compris*, I suppose). The proprietor's prompt answer to this was the French for "Nothing doing". The rich American had to go somewhere else. I like to think that even if he had offered a thousand dollars he would have had to go somewhere else. There are a few things in this proud Democracy (1100 miles southwest of Greece) that

American money cannot buy.

All this, I hope, may give you a rambling idea of my two favorite guidebooks in French. A definitive article covering the whole field of guidebooks would be a monstrous undertaking, and I hope nobody ever tries it. If anybody ever does, maybe he will summarize for me a large volume, published in England, which I picked up and put down in a bookstore one day. It is called "Aldor's 1937 in Europe" and a note on the cover announces that in it "thirty-seven writers guide you through twenty-seven countries". "It is bad enough," said a certain lady to me, apropos of this book, "to have one writer guide you through one country."

3

A RIDE WITH OLYMPY

Olympy Sementzoff called me "*Monsieur*" because I was the master of the Villa Tamisier and he was the gardener, the Russian husband of the French caretaker, Maria. I called him "*Monsieur*", too, because I could never learn to call any man Olympy and because there was a wistful air of *ancien régime* about him. He drank Bénédictine with me and smoked my cigarettes; he also, as you will see, drove my car. We conversed in French, a language alien to both of us, but more alien to me than to him. He said "*gauche*" for both "right" and "left" when he was upset, but when I was upset I was capable of flights that put the French people on their guard, wide-eyed and wary. Once, for instance, when I cut my wrist on a piece of glass I ran into the lobby of a hotel shouting in French, "I am sick with a knife!" Olympy would have known what to say (except that it would have been his left wrist in any case) but he wouldn't have shouted: his words ran softly together and sounded something like the burbling of water over stones.

Often I did not know what he was talking about; rarely did he know what I was talking about. There was a misty, faraway quality about this relationship, in French, of Russia and Ohio. The fact that the accident Olympy and I were involved in fell short of catastrophe was, in view of everything, something of a miracle.

Olympy and Maria "came with" the villa my wife and I rented on Cap d'Antibes. Maria was a deep-bosomed, large-waisted woman, as persistently pleasant as Riviera weather in a good season; no mistral ever blew in the even climate of her temperament. She must have been more than forty-five but she was as strong as a root; once when I had trouble getting a tough cork out of a wine bottle she took hold and whisked it out as if it had been a maidenhair fern. On Sundays her son came over from the barracks in Antibes and we all had a glass of white Bordeaux together, sometimes the Sementzoffs' wine, sometimes our own. Her son was eighteen and a member of the Sixth Regiment of Chasseurs Alpins, a tall, somber boy, handsome in his uniform and cape. He was an *enfant du premier lit,* as the French say. Maria made her first bed with a sergeant of the army who was *cordonnier* for his regiment during the war and seemed somehow to have laid by quite a little money. After the war the sergeant-shoemaker resigned from the army, put his money in investments of some profoundly mysterious nature in Indo-China, and lost it all. "*Il est mort,*" Maria told us, "*de chagrin.*" Grief over his ill-fortune brought on a decline; the *chagrin,* Maria said, finally reached his brain, and he died at the age of thirty-eight. Maria had to sell their house to pay the taxes, and go to work.

Olympy Sementzoff, Maria's second husband, was shy, not very tall, and wore a beard; in his working clothes you didn't notice much more than that. When he was dressed for Sunday – he wore a fine double-breasted jacket – you observed that his mouth was sensitive, his eyes attractively sad, and that he wore his shyness with a certain air. He worked in a boat factory over near Cannes –Maria said that he was a *spécialiste de bateaux;* odd jobs about the villa grounds he did on his off days. It was scarcely light when he got up in the morning, for he had to be at work at seven; it was almost dark when he got home. He was paid an incredibly small amount for what he did at the factory and a handful of sous each month for what he did about the grounds. When I gave him a hundred francs for some work he had done for me in the house – he could repair anything from a drain to a watch – he said, *"Oh, monsieur, c'est trop!"* *"Mais non, monsieur,"* said I. *"Ce n'est pas beaucoup."* He took it finally, after an exchange of bows and compliments.

The elderly wife of the Frenchman from whom we rented the villa told us, in a dark whisper, that Olympy was a White Russian and that there was perhaps a *petit mystère* about him, but we figured this as her own fanciful bourgeois alarm. Maria did not make a mystery out of her husband. There was the Revolution, most of Olympy's brothers and sisters were killed – one knew how that was – and he escaped. He was, of course, an exile and must not go back. If she knew just who he was in Russia and what he had done, she didn't make it very clear. He was in Russia and he escaped; she had married him thirteen years before; *et puis, voilà!* It would have been nice to believe that there was the blood of the Czars in Olympy, but if there was anything to the ancient legend that all the stray members of the Imperial House took easily and naturally to driving a taxi, that let Olympy out. He was not a born chauffeur, as I found out the day I came back from our automobile ride on foot and – unhappily for Maria – alone.

Olympy Sementzoff rode to and from his work in one of those bastard agglomerations of wheels, motor and superstructure that one saw only in France. It looked at first glance like the cockpit of a cracked-up plane. Then you saw that there were two wheels in front and a single wheel in back. Except for the engine – which Maria said was a "Morgan *moteur*" – and the wheels and tires, it was handmade. Olympy's boss at the boat factory had made most of it, but Olympy himself had put on the *ailes*, or fenders, which were made of some kind of wood. The strange canopy that served as a top was Maria's proud handiwork; it seemed to have been made of canvas and kitchen aprons. The thing had a right-hand drive. When the *conducteur* was in his seat he was very low to the ground: you had to bend down to talk to him. There was a small space beside the driver in which another person could sit, or crouch. The whole affair was not much larger than an overturned cabinet victrola. It got bouncingly under way with all the racket of a dog fight and in full swing was capable of perhaps thirty miles an hour. The contraption had cost Olympy three thousand francs, or about a hundred dollars. He had driven it for three years and was hand in glove with its mysterious mechanism. The gadgets on the dash and on the floorboard, which he pulled or pushed to make the thing go, seemed to include fire tongs, spoons, and doorknobs. Maria miraculously managed to squeeze into the seat beside the driver in an emergency, but I could understand why she didn't want to drive to the Nice Carnival in the "Morgan". It was because she didn't that I suggested Olympy should take her over one day in my Ford sedan. Maria had given us to understand that her *mari* could drive any car – he could be a chauffeur if he wanted to, a *bon* chauffeur. All I would have to do, *voyez-vous*, was to take Olympy for a turn around the Cap so that he could get the hang of the big car. Thus it was that one day after lunch we set off.

Half a mile out of Antibes on the shore road, I stopped the car and changed places with Olympy, letting the engine run. Leaning forward, he took a tense grip on a steering wheel much larger than he was used to and too far away from him. I could see that he was nervous. He put his foot on the clutch, tentatively, and said, *"Embrayage?"* He had me there. My knowledge of French automotive terms is inadequate and volatile. I was forced to say I didn't know. I couldn't remember the word for clutch in any of the three languages, French, Italian and German, in which it was given in my "Motorist's Guide" (which was back at the villa). Somehow *"embrayage"* didn't sound right for clutch (it is, though). I knew it wouldn't do any good for an American writer to explain in French to a Russian boat specialist the purpose that particular pedal served; furthermore, I didn't really know. I compromised by putting my left foot on the brake. *"Frein,"* I said. *"Ah,"* said Olympy, unhappily. This method of indicating what something might be by demonstrating what it wasn't had a disturbing effect. I shifted my foot to the accelerator – or rather pointed my toe at it – and suddenly the word for that, even the French for gasoline, left me. I was growing a little nervous myself. *"Benzina,"* I said, in Italian, finally. *"Ah?"* said Olympy. Whereas we had been one remove from reality to begin with, we were now two, or perhaps three, removes. A polyglot approach to the fine precision of a gas engine is roundabout and dangerous. We both lost a little confidence in each other. I suppose we should have given up right then, but we didn't.

Olympy decided the extra pedal was the *embrayage*, shifted into low from neutral, and the next thing I knew we were making a series of short forward bounds like a rabbit leaping out of a wheat field to see where he is. This form of locomotion takes a lot out of man and car. The engine complained in loud, rhythmic whines. And then Olympy somehow got his left foot on the starter and there was a familiar undertone of protest; this set his right foot to palpitating on the accelerator and the rabbit-jumps increased in scope. Abandoning my search for the word for starter, I grabbed his left knee and shouted *"Ça commence!"* Just what was commencing Olympy naturally couldn't figure – probably some habitual and ominous idiosyncrasy of the machinery. He gave me a quick, pale look. I shut off the ignition, and we discussed the starter situation, breathing a little heavily. He understood what it was, finally, and presently we were lurching ahead again,

Olympy holding her in low gear, like a wrestler in a clinch, afraid to risk shifting into second. He tried it at last and with a jamming jolt and a roar we went into reverse: the car writhed like a tortured leopard and the engine quit.

I was puzzled and scared, and so was Olympy. Only a foolish pride in masculine fortitude kept us going. I showed him the little jog to the right you have to make to shift into second and he started the engine and we were off again, jolting and lurching. He made the shift, finally, with a noise like lightning striking a foundry – and veered swoopingly to the right. We barely missed a series of staunch granite blocks, set in concrete, that mark ditches and soft shoulders. We whisked past a pole. The leaves of a vine hanging on a wall slapped at me through the window. My voice left me. I was fascinated and paralyzed by the swift passes disaster was making at my head. At length I was able to grope blindly toward the ignition switch, but got my wrist on the klaxon button. When I jerked my arm away, Olympy began obediently sounding the horn. We were riding on the edge of a ditch. I managed somehow to shut off the ignition and we rolled to a stop. Olympy, unused to a left-hand drive, had forgotten there was a large portion of the car to his right, with me in it. I told him, *"A gauche, à gauche, toujours à gauche!"* "Ah," said Olympy, but there was no comprehension in him. I could see he didn't know we had been up against the vines of villa walls: intent on the dark problem of gearshifting, he had been oblivious of where the car and I had been. There was a glint in his eye now. He was determined to get the thing into high on his next attempt; we had come about half a mile in the lower gears.

The road curved downhill as it passed Eden Roc and it was here that an elderly English couple, unaware of the fact that hell was loose on the highway, were walking. Olympy was in second again, leaning forward like a racing bicycle rider. I shouted at him to look out, he said *"Oui"* – and we grazed the old man and his wife. I glanced back in horror: they were staring at us, mouths and eyes wide, unable to move or make a sound. Olympy raced on to a new peril: a descending hairpin curve, which he negotiated in some far-fetched manner, with me hanging onto the emergency brake. The road straightened out, I let go the brake, and Olympy slammed into high with the desperate gesture of a man trying to clap his hat over a poised butterfly. We began to whiz: Olympy hadn't counted on a fast pickup. He whirled around a car in front of us with a foot to spare. *"Lentement!"* I shouted, and then *"Gauche!"* as I began to get again the whimper of poles and walls in my ears. *"Ça va mieux, maintenant,"* said Olympy, quietly. A wild thought ran through my head that maybe this was the way they used to drive in Russia in the old days.

Ahead of us now was one of the most treacherous curves on the Cap. The road narrowed and bent, like a croquet wicket, around a high stone wall that shut off your view of what was coming. What was coming was usually on the wrong side of the road, so it wouldn't do to shout *"Gauche!"* now. We made the turn all right. There was a car coming, but it was well over on its own side. Olympy apparently didn't think so. He whirled the wheel to the right, didn't take up the play fast enough in whirling it back, and there was a tremendous banging crash, like a bronze monument falling. I had a glimpse of Olympy's right hand waving around like the hand of a man hunting for something under a table. I didn't know what his feet were doing. We were still moving, heavily, with a ripping noise and a loud roar. "*Poussez le phare!*" I shouted, which means "push the headlight!" "*Ah-h-h-h,*" said Olympy. I shut off the ignition and pulled on the hand brake, but we had already stopped. We got out and looked at the pole we had sideswiped and at the car. The right front fender was crumpled and torn and the right back one banged up, but nothing else had been hurt. Olympy's face was so stricken when he looked at me that I felt I had to cheer him up. "*Il fait beau,*" I announced, which is to say that the weather is fine. It was all I could think of.

I started for a garage that Olympy knew about. At the first street we came to he said "*Gauche*" and I turned left. "*Ah, non,*" said Olympy. "*Gauche,*" and he pointed the other way. "You mean *droit?*" I asked, just that way. "*Ah!*" said Olympy. "*C'est bien ça!*" It was as if he had thought of something he hadn't been able to remember for days. That explained a great deal.

I left Olympy and the car at the garage; he said he would walk back. One of the garage men drove me into Juan-les-Pins and I walked home from there – and into a look of wild dismay in Maria's eyes. I hadn't thought about that: she had seen us drive away together and here I was, alone. "*Où est votre mari?*" I asked her, hurriedly. It was something of a failure as a reassuring beginning. I had taken the question out of her own mouth, so I answered it. "He has gone for a walk," I told her. Then I tried to say that her husband was *bon*, but I pronounced it *beau*, so that what I actually said was that her husband was handsome. She must have figured that he was not only dead but laid out. There was a *mauvais quart d'heure* for both of us before the drooping figure of Olympy finally appeared. He explained sadly to Maria that the mechanism of the Ford is strange and curious compared to the mechanism of the Morgan. I agreed with him. Of course, he protested, he would pay for the repairs to the car, but Maria and I both put down that suggestion. Maria's idea of my work was that I was paid by the City of New York and enjoyed a tremendous allowance. Olympy got forty francs a day at the boat factory.

That night, at dinner, Maria told us that her *mari* was pacing up and down in their little bedroom at the rear of the house. He was in a state. I didn't want an attack of *chagrin* to come on him as it had on the *cordonnier* and perhaps reach his brain. When Maria was ready to go we gave her a handful of cigarettes for Olympy and a glass of Bénédictine. The next day, at dawn, I heard the familiar *tintamarre* and *hurlement* and *brouhaha* of Olympy's wonderful contraption getting under way once more. He was off to the boat factory and his forty francs a day, his dollar and thirty cents. It would have cost him two weeks' salary to pay for the fenders, but he would have managed it somehow. When I went down to breakfast, Maria came in from the kitchen with a large volume, well fingered and full of loose pages, which she handed to me. It was called

Le Musée d'Art and subtitled *Galerie des Chefs-d'oeuvre et Précis de l'Histoire de l'Art au XIX Siècle, en France et à l'Etranger (1000 gravures, 58 planches hors texte).* A present to *Monsieur* from Olympy Sementzoff, with his compliments. The incident of the automobile was thus properly rounded off with an exchange of presents: cigarettes, Bénédictine, and *Le Musée d'Art.* It seemed to me the way such things should always end, but perhaps Olympy and I were ahead of our day – or behind it.

4

AN AFTERNOON IN PARIS

Twelve great avenues – I suppose all Parisian children can recite their names – march in bright and clamorous dignity out of that tremendous circle called the Place de l'Etoile, of which the Arc de Triomphe marks the impressive and precise center. The avenues lead to the twelve corners and the twelve thousand wonders of Paris. I am sure there must be many a tourist who, losing his hotel in a swirl of *rues*, has to hunt up the Place de l'Etoile in order to orient himself. Conversely, it is also as easy a place as any in the world to step off into bewilderment and confusion. Take the Avenue Hoche, instead of the Avenue Foch, by mistake, and where are you? Well, in a few minutes you are in the Parc Monceau instead of the Bois de Boulogne – and if it was in the Bois de Boulogne that your wife and her mother made you promise to meet them for tea, you are hopelessly lost.

I first saw the Place de l'Etoile on a rainy day in November, 1918, just a few weeks before half a million people jammed the circle and the streets round about and shouted, "*Vive Veelson!*" as the Savior of Democracy rode grandly by on his steep way down from the Pinnacle of Fame – or, at any rate, from the Heights of Popularity. My accustomed route in those days was in the direction of the Seine by way of the Avenue d'Iéna, which led into a *quartier* that was then *bien américain*. First you came to the little Place des Etats-Unis, where, at No. 11, Woodrow Wilson was to live during his months in Paris. From the second-floor windows of No. 11 one can see the statue of Washington and Lafayette (they are shaking hands) that was presented to the city of Paris by Joseph Pulitzer in 1895. At the other end of the square, under the chestnut trees, there has stood since 1923 the monument to the Americans who died in the Lafayette Escadrille, the Foreign Legion, and the American Field Service. A little farther along the Avenue d'Iéna you come to the Rue Freycinet, which drops down quickly to the Rue de Chaillot, in which, at No. 5, the chancellery of the American Embassy was housed in those days (it has since been moved to a magnificent new building in the Place de la Concorde). In front of the *ancien* chancellery the figure of Jean Baptiste Donatien de Vimeur, Comte de Rochambeau, raises his right hand as if in salute to the equestrian statue of George Washington, a hundred yards farther on, in the place d'Iéna. Washington holds a sword aloft, and I have heard it said that this sword had to be replaced half a dozen times during the Peace Conference days because American doughboys and gobs were forever climbing up on the horse and wrenching the blade loose for a souvenir.

The streets of this neighborhood were loud with Americans in the months after the war, for in addition to the chancellery, the American Navy Headquarters were just around the corner. United States Marines used to play catch and knock out flies in the Place d'Iéna to the amazement of the French populace (*"C'est bizarre, ça!"*) and the annoyance – as fruitless as it was vehement – of the police. You could hear "How Y' Gonna Keep 'Em Down on the Farm?" and "Mademoiselle from Armentière" and "Smiles". Soldiers and sailors, secretaries of the Embassy, stenographers, and code clerks made the district as American as Pennsylvania Avenue. They all departed long ago, of course; the chancellery, as I said, has moved, and the doors you went through to reach the Navy Headquarters now lead into a quiet bar called the Pamela, which wistfully advertises in its window Side Cars and Manhattans and Bronxes, but dispenses, I am sure, mainly Pernod and *vermouth-cassis*. Baseballs fly no more, the streets no longer ring with song, Washington's sword is safe; the region has been tranquilly captured again by the French. I spent an afternoon there in 1937 searching for old landmarks, renewing one or two old acquaintances, finding, to be sure, a few changes.

A stone tablet, erected by the Paris Post of the American Legion a few years ago at No. 5 Rue de Chaillot (where for a year and a half I labored, or at least fiddled around, as a code clerk), interested me. It reads, "In memory of Myron T. Herrick – 1854-1929. Served his country during the World War as American Ambassador to the French Republic." The word "during" here has the force of "throughout" and is quite misleading. I am sure, however, that the imprecision rose out of ignorance rather than malice – malice, I mean, toward the Hon. William G. Sharp of Elyria, Ohio, who served his country during all but the first four months of the World War as American Ambassador to the French Republic. And even during those four months, from August to December, 1914, Mr. Sharp was technically, if not actually, the American Ambassador to France. The experienced Mr. Herrick had been kept on, after his time, by request of the French government, as I remember it; Mr. Sharp toyed restlessly with his credentials in a suite in a hotel. When, at the end of the four months, Mr. Herrick turned over the Embassy to Mr. Sharp, the former had already become forever famous as the American War Ambassador to France. History moved out of No. 5 Rue de Chaillot with Myron Herrick, leaving to William Sharp a little corner of oblivion.

During the brief weeks that Herrick anomalously tarried, a Republican Ambassador under a Democratic President, the Germans drove so hard upon Paris that the French government retreated to Bordeaux, and many a foreign representative packed up and left, too. Mr. Herrick stayed bravely on. So, although no mention was made of it, did Mr. Sharp. It was reported in the French and American press that Herrick, urged to flee to safety, had gloriously said, "Sometimes a dead Ambassador can be of greater service to his country than a live one." Mr. Herrick, research has shown, did not say those words at all; they would appear to have been invented by some harried journalist hunting for a striking lead to a story. Nevertheless, they helped enormously to make Mr. Herrick's fame, as legend (cf. "Lafayette, we are here") always does. There can be no doubt that Mr. Herrick was a gallant gentleman and that he worked arduously and late at the Embassy before he surrendered his desk to his successor. But he was never in any greater danger of death than Mr. Sharp. The latter, unfortunately for his fame, was not a brilliant or forceful man. He lacked Herrick's engaging courtliness and winning manner. He did not pronounce, nor did anyone pronounce for him, any gallant sayings during 1915, 1916, 1917, and 1918. He just muddled through, an Ohio businessman who, for some obscure reason, had always wanted to be Ambassador to France. In one of his labored and pedestrian dispatches to the State Department he reported that a German shell had landed one day in a street only three blocks from the chancellery and had killed a white horse. That dispatch has remained a little joke of the service. But it is interesting to note that no German shell ever landed that close to Myron T. Herrick. William Sharp retired because of ill health in 1919 and died shortly afterward. Nobody much remembers him. There is no memorial to him in Paris that I know of – beyond a few amusing and persistent little anecdotes. He remains *le grand inconnu* of the American diplomatic service.

There is, of course, a memorial to Woodrow Wilson in that very section of Paris I have been talking about. This is the Avenue du Président Wilson, which crosses the Place d'Iéna just a few steps behind the statue of Washington. It was named in his honor when he was in the heyday of his popularity, but I have no doubt that if the French could quietly change the name now, without causing hard feelings, they would do so; it would probably become the Avenue Gaston Doumergue tomorrow. It seems to me significant that the house in which Wilson lived, at No.11 Place des Etats-Unis, bears no marker of any kind. I would not have known how to find it on the day of my ramble – for there are a great many huge stone houses on the Place, all looking very much alike – if it had not been for M. Léon Barthélémy.

I first knew M. Barthélémy in 1918. He was the head *coiffeur* – indeed, the *gérant* – of a barbershop in the Avenue Kléber, just up the Rue Boissière from the Place d'Iéna, where I used to go to get my hair cut. Once, in those days, when I did not find him at his chair and inquired where he was, I was proudly told that he had gone to cut the hair of President Wilson at his house in the Place des Etats-Unis. Later, the little, black-haired *coiffeur* was all smiles when he announced to me that the President had indeed honored him by selecting him as his special barber in Paris. But I was not to believe this was his first great client. He had had princes and generals and premiers in his day; *Son Excellence, Monsieur le Président,* was simply the *greatest* of his clients.

In 1925, back in Paris after six years, I looked up M. Barthélémy – and there he was, still doing business at the old stand. Woodrow Wilson, the greatest of his clients, had now become the greatest of his idols. He told me what they used to talk about – they talked in English, because the great man's French was not too good – but I have forgotten what it was. And did I know that he, Léon Barthélémy, had cut the hair of Kerensky, also? Kerensky, I was to understand, was the most nervous client he had ever had – although he had had a great many nervous clients – for he was constantly jumping up whenever a door slammed or a motor backfired or a manicurist dropped a pair of scissors; he thought "they" were sneaking up on him, taking pot shots, throwing bombs. I wrote a little story about M. Barthélémy and it was printed in the old Sunday *World*.

In my wanderings I thought of M. Barthélémy. I walked again up the Rue Boissière to the Avenue Kléber, with doubt and misgiving, for it had been twelve years since I had seen the little barber last, and almost twenty since I had first entered his shop. I was afraid his place would be gone, and it is sad to find places which you once frequented in Paris no longer there. But not a single thing about the little shop had changed; even the small barber pole up above the door, with its red and white stripes topped by white stars on a field of blue, was still there. And so was Léon Barthélémy, as dark-haired (amazingly) as ever, as smiling, and as full of his memories of Woodrow Wilson. But, I must know, he had had Papa Joffre as a client in his last days, and frequently made a trip to a place near Versailles to visit the widow of the great *Maréchal*. We talked of all his famous clients for a while. Then I told him I wanted to be sure which house it was that Wilson had lived in. "I will go with you," he said, "and we will see it together." So he took off his smock and put on his hat, and we made the little pilgrimage and he pointed to the high, wide window on the second floor at No.11 out of which the President used to look when he was having his hair trimmed. A French family of wealth lives in No.11 now, the *coiffeur* thought.

He walked with me the length of the pretty park that forms the center of the Place des Etats-Unis, to look at the monument to the Americans who died in the service of France during the war, one hundred and eighteen in all, sixty-one of them in the Lafayette Escadrille. Their names are all carved in granite, with the usual number of mistakes that the French invariably make in dealing with Anglo-American proper names. John is occasionally spelled Johu, etc. Raoul Lufbery – on the spelling of which you can catch many an American – is right, and so are the names of Norman Prince, and Kiffin Rockwell, and Alan Seeger, and most of the others. I noticed that the name of Warren Hobbs appears twice, and so does that of Ely Dinsmore, or Dinsmore Ely – I am sorry I don't know which one is correct, for it is carved both ways. A little French boy came up and began marking on the monument with a piece of chalk, and my friend told him to stop, in a burst of indignation. "*Pardon*," said the little boy, and ran away.

I walked back toward M. Barthélémy's shop a little way with my companion because I had one more call to make. There used to be a Madame Rocagel who kept a cleaning-and-pressing shop on the Avenue Kléber. I had taken my suits there to be pressed in 1918 and 1919, and I had always liked her. She was *gracieuse* and she complimented me on my ungainly French, and I used to stay and try it out on her. She had been then a woman of perhaps fifty. Her daughter, a pretty girl of fourteen, had helped her in the shop, studying English in her spare time and practising it on me once in a while when I called and found her alone. I had dropped in to see Madame Rocagel and Marie in 1925, and Madame had been there, but her daughter was away. Now once again, I found Madame alone – very gray, seventy, as gracious as ever, still carrying on. We talked about the old days. She assured me my French was remarkable (perhaps she meant *incroyable*). I asked about Marie – had she married? *Oh, mais non*. Marie was out somewhere, shopping, or reading a book in a park. Madame asked me to have a glass of Malaga with her, but I was running out of phrases, so I left, with my best bow.

Marie, I calculated on my way back toward the Place de l'Etoile, must be all of thirty-three now. I wondered if she was still pretty. I wondered how good her English was after nineteen years. Thirty-three! It was difficult to think of her as anything except the eager, dark-eyed little girl of fourteen who used to try so hard, so blushingly, and with such a charming accent, to say "th" the way I said it. Thirty-three! I found myself getting leg-weary, and I hailed a cab before I got to the Arch. Paris, I thought as I climbed into the cab, may never change, as the saying goes – but people do. I'm not as young as I once was, myself.

5

LA GRANDE VILLE DE PLAISIR

There is an old saying that if Paris had a street like La Canebière it would be a little Marseilles, to which I shall add that if Marseilles had a Promenade des Anglais it would be a little Nice. Marseilles is famous for the dark dangers of its back streets and for mysterious doings along its waterfront. Just the other day boxes containing six thousand gold watches, in transit from Geneva to Buenos Aires, were eased of their treasure and magically filled with chunks of cement on a quay in Marseilles. You may have read about that: the police news of Marseilles has a habit of getting on the international press wires. The activities of lawbreakers in Nice, on the other hand, may often be read about only in the local papers, of which my favorite is the enormously interesting *L'Eclaireur de Nice et du Sud-Est*. The *voleurs* of Nice take, as a rule, one watch at a time, or one wallet, but they frequently manage it in a picturesque fashion.

If you should see a fat and jovial priest drop a well-filled billfold behind him on the Promenade, return it to him, bow politely, wink and proceed on your way. Tarry not to make an acquaintance that will show rapid signs of ripening into a pleasant and perhaps profitable companionship. The dropped wallet is the opening move in an ancient swindle that works like a charm in this friendly climate. When I was in Nice twelve years ago the wolves in priests' clothing (sometimes it was in the clothing of retired philanthropists or bankers) reaped, as the saying goes, a rich harvest. I remember a professor of economics in a Pennsylvania college who waited for three hours in a café for his old pal the priest to show up. This particular variant of the venerable racket had begun with a most interesting talk about faith in one's fellow-man and had ended by the professor agreeing to prove his own faith in his fellow-man by allowing the priest to walk around the block with his (the professor's) wallet. Usually the old game is worked with considerably more subtlety; often several enjoyable weeks drift by before the holy father (or the philanthropist or the banker) feels the fruit is ripe enough for the plucking. Always in the end a gentleman of great faith is left sitting in a café, or a hotel room, looking anxiously at his wristwatch (unless, of course, he has lent that to his good friend, too). In the winter of 1925 the Riviera edition of the Chicago *Tribune*, for which I was a reporter, ran every day on its front page a warning about the swindlers; it didn't seem to do much good.

The general run of waywardness in Nice may be on a lesser scale than that of Marseilles, but it is infinitely more fascinating. *Inconnus* are found mysteriously injured, *malheureux* get into all kinds of curious difficulties, *indéli-cats* are found wandering around with nothing on. If you have to keep your ear to the ground and your eye on the *Eclaireur* to learn about them, it is partly because Nice is a carnival city whose daily news is drowned in a trumpeting of ballyhoo and a showering of confetti. The *Syndicate d'Initiative* and the Rotary Club – surely the strongest outside the United States – and the other organizations that go in for rosy pictures of this *grande ville de plaisir* dwell so loudly on the climate and the carnival that the casual visitor would not imagine anything out of the way ever happened here. And yet, like another Poictesme, it is a place in which almost anything is more than likely to happen. The night I arrived in the city recently a *malheureux* ran across the Place Masséna bleeding copiously from a cut throat and gurgling, *"Je vais mourir!"* (He didn't die, however.) The next night a man scurried past me hotly pursued by a woman who kept screaming "Police!" (Nobody paid any attention.)

It is always with a sense of high expectation that I set out into the city. If the day's excitement doesn't break actually about my head, I can always read about it in the *Eclaireur*. At 2:30 yesterday afternoon (I see by the paper before me), in the Rue Barla, an Algerian named Tayeb Mihoubi was stabbed by a Moroccan named Mohamed ben Mohamed; one Mme. Grocorini, having irked a gentleman named Valerio Franchi, was slashed by the gentleman's knife and when a M. Ricci rashly intervened, he was slashed, too. Knives rise and fall on this lovely littoral as easily and for as little provocation as a woman's tears. There are thousands of Italians and Corsicans in Nice, and a great scattering of Algerians, Moroccans, and somber dark men from a dozen other countries. The city has been a place of sojourn and foray ever since it was founded by the Phocaeans twenty centuries ago; it has been overrun by Ligurians, Celts, Romans, Saracens, Englishmen, and Americans. It has a tradition of restlessness.

One of the most remarkable manifestations of the restlessness of Nice and the surrounding country is the *bagarre*. *Bagarre* means "violent disorder, uproar, crush, squabble, scuffle, fray". Today's *Eclaireur* tells of the final disposition, in the courts, of a famous *bagarre*, more exactly known as "*La Fusillade de la Place Arson*", which took place as long ago as August, 1936 (the wheels of justice turn slowly in the south). As is usually the case with *bagarres*, nobody knows exactly how or why this one started, but it had something to do with politics. In the end scores of men were involved and more than two hundred shots were fired. Nobody was killed or even seriously injured, which the *Eclaireur* admits it is at a loss to understand, and so am I. Most of the shooting took place at close quarters; there must have been a kind of carnival touch about so much spectacular and aimless gunfire. Anyway, the case has been finally disposed of: eight men were fined twenty-five francs each, or less than a dollar, for illegal possession of firearms. That was all. The *Eclaireur* intimates that it was not considered discreet to prosecute the defendants on any more serious or relevant charges. Such a procedure, one gathers, could easily start a *bagarre* all over again – perhaps right there in the courtroom.

Of recent *bagarres*, the one that has interested me most took place in a village a few miles from Nice, but since it was of the very scheme and rhythm of many a similar happening within the city's limits, I must report it. It will give you as clear an idea as may be had of what a *bagarre* is like. The *Eclaireur* launches into the puzzling story in this manner: "In spite of promises given, in spite of appeals for calm, the closing of the Institute of Actinology was not accomplished without incident." I do not know what an institute of actinology is or why it should be difficult to close one without incident; probably anywhere else in the world it would be child's play to close an institute of actinology. But not in Nice or vicinity. It was the Messrs. Mandouce, Guenon, and Billet, and a Mme. Veran, who tried to close this one. M. Guenon was immediately set upon by a young man named Roba, who was accompanied by the Messrs. Lanteri, Bernardi, and Grindou. M. Roba beat M. Guenon savagely about the head, either with a rock or a *poing américan* (brass knuckles). A M. Monti drifted into the scuffle from somewhere, rescued M. Guenon, and took him to a doctor, who bandaged his wounds. Afterward, M. Guenon went to a café run by a M. Laugier and was having a glass of something to steady his nerves when one Vincent Martino entered, saw the injured man's bandages, and asked him what had happened. Before he could get a reply, M. Martino was punched in the head by a M. Baracco. From here on the story loses its sharp clarity. M. Martino whipped out a gun, but hastily hid it in a cardboard box when a police-

man entered. M. Guenon and M. Baracco drop quietly out
of the tortured narrative at this point, but M. Martino was
led off to the police station. That didn't cause things to
quiet down. "A crowd of three hundred people gathered
about the café," says the *Eclaireur,* "shouting and gesticulating. Women mingled in the crowd, also shouting and
gesticulating." Presently some cops shouldered their way
through the mob, not to restore order, it turns out, but to
hunt for M. Martino's gun, which the first *agent* had
neglected to seize. They found the gun and went away.
The crowd stayed and grew increasingly menacing as the
night wore on, so that M. Laugier finally had to close the
café. We learn that the police investigations went on late
into the night, but just what angles of the involved case
they were investigating is not made clear; I have an idea,
though, they were concentrating on M. Martino's gun.
The *Eclaireur* ends the story with this musical sentence:
"*Dans la rue, le calme est long à revenir.*" That, then, is a
typical *bagarre,* violent, cloudy, complicated. It is no use
trying to fit the incidents together into a logical pattern.
The *Eclaireur* and the police gave that up long ago. And so
did I.

There is an embarrassing richness of clippings before
me, cut from the *Eclaireurs* of only one week. Several
standing headlines recur frequently, one of them the
simple phrase "*Les Pochards*". A *pochard* is a drunk. The
headline has something of the slangy, sardonic force of
"Among the Soused" or "With the Cockeyed". The
stories deal briefly with the activities of gentlemen who,
while in their cups, have caused a slight "scandal" here, a

mild "outrage" there. Another headline, "*Les Conducteurs Imprudents et Maladroits*", tops almost every day a considerable list of automobile accidents. I note that just yesterday a big Hispano-Suiza sports roadster, driven by a baron, knocked down a lamp-post on the Promenade des Anglais and that shortly afterward another *imprudent* knocked down a palm tree. The Promenade is more dangerous than the Place de la Concorde. I remember that when I was here before, the *Eclaireur* ran a picture of a Promenade traffic cop who was in the hospital for no less than the seventh time as the result of having been knocked down by a motorist on that broad thoroughfare.

My clippings deal with a dozen other varied and spectacular episodes, but I shall go into detail only about the curious case of M. Antoine Semeria, aged 47, a *mécanicien-dentiste*, because it is typical of a special class of bizarre goings on in this Paradise on the Bay of the Angels. M. Semeria was dragged up before M. Giocanti, *commissaire* of police, because he had refused to pay his fare on an autobus. He explained to the *commissaire* that it was his invariable custom not to pay for riding on autobuses. Ride on them he would, pay he would not, and that was that – the *commissaire* would see. M. Giocanti listened patiently for a while and then directed that M. Semeria be put away in a hospital for observation. M. Semeria was placed in the hospital, escaped immediately, boarded the first bus that came along, once more refused to pay, and was hauled up before the *commissaire* again before you could say Giocanti.

I have touched on only one or two special phases of the

rich life of this great, colorful city of almost 250,000 inhabitants (not counting the visitors, who nearly double the permanent population) that sprawls between the mountains and the sea. Up on the hill back of the town is the old Roman quarter called Cimiez, where Queen Victoria stayed, a region almost as sedate and quiet as it was in her time, but considerably more crowded. From the heights above the city you can look down on a panorama as diverse as life itself: the streets of the shopkeepers and the bourgeoisie in the more modern part of town; the narrow *rues* of the Vieille-Ville down by the sea, where the Italians live; the *faubourg* of the Port of Nice, which visitors rarely get to; and the region around the Place Masséna (*"centre de l'animation, coeur de la ville"*), which visitors seldom get away from. The main thoroughfare of the tourist's quarter is, of course, the Promenade des Anglais. It was in hotels along this boulevard that Isadora Duncan, Rudolph Valentino, Harry Sinclair, and Papa Laemmle lived when I was here before. In those four you have a colored-postcard picture of this *centre de vie joyeuse* in the gay days before the depression. It was an exciting winter, the winter of 1925. Nowadays I more or less wander around, an outsider on a visit, but that season I was in the midst of the excitement.

I think it was the Hôtel Ruhl et Anglais that I called up the night, twelve years ago, when a wire came to us on the *Tribune* saying that Serge Yessenin, Isadora Duncan's former husband, had killed himself in Moscow. I was directed to get the great lady on the phone and find out what she had to say (it sometimes seemed to me that this nasty business of interviewing bereaved women was what editors figured me to be cut out for in my days as a newspaperman). The hotel reported that Miss Duncan was out and was not expected back before one o'clock in the morning. At a little after one (ours was a morning newspaper) I got her on the phone. It came out that she had not yet heard about the death of the man with whom she had once led such a tumultuous life. I am sure I must have managed it all very badly; I was scared. I remember that she said nothing but "No, no, no, no," which she repeated a dozen times, and that finally she let the receiver fall. I called back the hotel, and speaking English to a puzzled French night clerk, shouted at him to do something about Miss Duncan. I have no idea what he did. I never saw Isadora Duncan. The next day, however, she granted interviews to other reporters and, according to the *Eclaireur*, told them she felt sure that the poem which Yessenin is reported to have written in his own blood before he died was a poem to her. It was, I believe, on the Promenade des Anglais of this violent city that Isadora Duncan met her tragic and implausible end when a scarf she was wearing trailed out of the car she was riding in, caught in a wheel, and choked her to death. I remember my phone call to Isadora Duncan all too clearly. I remember, too, how indestructibly healthy Valentino, who had only a few months to live, looked. And how Harry Sinclair, consenting warily to an interview, never once met my gaze but stared at me out of the corner of his right eye.

Nobody, however, so surely typified for me the faintly

sinister fascination of this ancient city of the Phocaeans as did a tall young Hindu who showed up silently and ominously in the little office of the *Tribune* one night. We had a week before advertised for a proof-reader who knew English and more than fifty persons had answered the ad, among them the young Hindu. They were an amazing group: a Belgian woman of seventy-five, a former captain in the British Army, a Russian prince, a Scotch teacher, a French painter, all sorts and conditions of drifters and dreamers – the flotsam of fifty nations that you can raise, with one signal or another, from Cimiez up on the hill to the steep streets of the old town by the sea. The editor had finally hired the former British Army man. But our Hindu, who appeared so softly out of the night, swore vehemently that it was he who had been hired. His dark stare was menacing, his perfect English had a dangerous edge. He was as straight-backed as a knife. "I have come for the job I was hired for," he said. "I am ready to start work." The editor, looking a little gray, said he had hired another man. "Oh, no, you haven't," said the Hindu quietly, and then shouted, "You hired me!" There was an unbearably long silence while he glared at each of us in turn. Then, suddenly turning on the editor again, he cried, "I know who you are and all about you! You are Lame-Leg Charlie, the dope fiend! Remember this – you haven't seen the last of me!" And the door somehow opened behind him and he was gone. The editor's name was not Charlie, he was not lame, and he didn't take dope. Our visitor's dark threat and his darker revelations, which were never cleared up, left us all a little shaken. It turned out that we *had* seen the last of our Hindu, but there was never a night that I didn't expect him to show up again to wreak whatever peculiar vengeance it is that frustrated Hindu proof-readers go in for. I put this story in because Nice is like that.

Nice is like this, too: One day in 1926 the mistral, that violent and unpredictable wind from the Alps, came to town, like a cavalcade of desperadoes drunk and firing from both hips. It knocked over chimneys, ripped off signs, tore shutters loose from windows. I was walking with a lady in the Avenue Félix-Faure when the terror descended. The lady walked, I am happy to say, very fast – so fast that we were able to step clear of fifty tons of bricks that suddenly roared and thundered to the pavement behind us. A high parapet surmounting a row of six one-story shops and forming a false second-story front had been toppled into the street by the wind hurricaning behind it. I can still see with too great clarity the hand of a man who was killed in the wreckage, sticking up out of his tomb of bricks. A few moments before, I had been abreast of him. The lady, as I have said, was a fast walker.

All this, then, past and present, is Nice, the capital of gaiety, the mother city of this bright shore of winter playgrounds. If I have made her seem perhaps a trifle too violent, I must make some amends. Nice has her quiet moments, her tranquil *quartiers*, she has even her proud memories of a holy visitation. It is nice to know as you walk past the trim façade of the Hôtel Beau-Rivage on the Quai des Etats-Unis that on a November day fifty years ago a certain obscure Frenchman named Martin decided to stay there one night with his two daughters, Céline and Thérèse. It is nice to know that from one of the wide windows Thérèse Martin looked out on the palm trees and the deep blue of the Bay of the Angels. It is an enchanting view. Who knows what high resolve it may not have inspired in the young girl who was to become perhaps the most beloved of all the saints in the calendar to the people of her country – Sainte Thérèse de l'Enfant Jésus, France's "Little Flower". Or you can walk into the peaceful old graveyard of the English Church of the Holy Trinity and ponder on the modest tombstone of a reverend English gentleman, Henry Francis Lyte, of Lower Brixham in Devon, whose prayer that he might "leave behind some blessing for his fellows, some fair trust to guide, to cheer, to elevate mankind" was answered in, of all places, Nice, where just before he died, in November, 1847, he was moved to write the surely immortal hymn that begins "Abide with me, fast falls the eventide".

Eventide in November falls very fast indeed in Nice. The darkness caught me one afternoon, two months ago, in the little graveyard, but not before I had seen the gleam of a small white card tacked to the church door. I went over to see if some fair trust might not be lettered on it. The living actuality of Nice abruptly overtook me, there in the gloaming, dispelling my mood of reverie. The card sadly announced that because of numerous thefts, the place of worship had to be kept locked; visitors were requested to ask the sexton for the key.

6

JOURNEY TO THE PYRENEES

The day after the Czechs shot the two Germans in the spring of 1938, we were in a service flat off Piccadilly, having driven up from Dover two days before through alternating patches of rain and hawthorn blossom, sunshine and hail. McCulloch brought up the morning papers with the toast and coffee and we read about the crisis. McCulloch looked worried. This, it came out, was only because he managed a building with eleven flats, all occupied, and illness among his servants had kept him understaffed. We talked about the drive up from Dover and about last year's weather – it hadn't rained once during the two weeks of Wimbledon. McCulloch said that if we should want tea later in the afternoon just to give him a ring.

After breakfast we walked through Hyde Park, which was crowded because it was a warm, sunny day. People were lying on the grass, sitting on chairs, playing with their dogs. The place was full of Scotties and spaniels and wire-haireds, chasing balls, barking at the swans. We idled along and caught the drift of conversations: about the shocking defeat of England by Switzerland in a soccer game at Zurich, about the dark outlook for the English Davis Cup team against the Yugoslavs at Zagreb. Nobody was talking about Czechoslovakia. It reminded me of Juan-les-Pins on the day after the Hitler coup in Vienna: the wistaria and the white iris had come into bloom, the weather was fine, and people were out in their brightest clothes, talking, about this and that, shouting at their children, playing with their dogs. It reminded me of the day we had driven into Luchon, too, on the edge of the Spanish war. This story is mainly about driving to Luchon and the quiet we ran into there.

The going in Gaul has vastly improved since the year 218 B.C. when Hannibal took a month to push his thirty-seven elephants from the valley of the Rhone to the pass of the Little Saint Bernard, on his celebrated journey from Cartagena to the outskirts of Rome. Nowadays on the fine French roads you could get from Juan-les-Pins to Luchon between sunrise and sunset, if you had to – and you wouldn't have to go as fast as Prince Bernhard of Holland who recently did ninety miles an hour between Cannes and Avignon, for the hell of it, burning out the bearings of his special racing car so that new ones had to be sent to him by plane from Rome. We took four days getting to Luchon – which is fast enough through this storied country.

There hadn't been any rain to speak of on Cap d'Antibes for months and people had been going to the little chapel of La Garoupe to pray for it. They weren't worried about war, they were worried about drought. The morning we started out the sky was cloudy but there was a south wind which Maria, cook and prophet, said would prevail and keep off the rain, prayers or no prayers. The gods crossed her up when we got into the Esterel; the wind shifted into the east and the Roman ruins in Fréjus were soaked when we passed through. The rain freshened up the white and purple lilacs – and the trolley tracks of Toulon, making them fine for skidding.

The motorists of Provence perpetuate the violent old traditions of this *beau pays*. One of them in Toulon tried to pass a moving trolley car on a wet, narrow street, banged into a curb, banged into the car, got tagged in the spare tire as he forged ahead onto the tracks, but managed to keep on going in a series of swooping skids. The driver and the wattman, as the French so wonderfully call motormen, kept shouting vilifications at each other throughout the whole scene. There is no fear can silence the indignant volubility of a French motorist – or even make him keep both hands on the wheel. The thing to do is stop when you sense these things happening, even a block away. Ours is another madness, set to a different rhythm, and no American can hope to comprehend the highly specialized patterns woven so suddenly and so magically on the shuttle of French roads. One should lie low when the French begin to bang into each other, and wait until the desperate design is disentangled and the highway is quiet again.

The roads of France are notable for their straightness and their sound surfacing. Outside of towns there are few blind crossings. You almost never see a pack of cars, nose to tail, chasing each other over the highways. Ten miles out of Paris in any direction you virtually have the road to yourself. But the French drive always at an angry rate of speed, they blow their horns wildly for crossings but never slow down, and their favorite sport is passing a car that's passing a car on a three-lane road. They recognize no courtesies of the road and are confused if you extend any. Thus it is that they can hold their own with any nation in number and quality of crackups.

Winding up back of Toulon, we got into moist spears of snow that turned to large lazy flakes on the mountain top. On the other side, in "true" Provence, we came down onto dry roads under a summer sun. Here you begin to see at the branching of highways the exciting names of Avignon and Tarascon and Beaucaire. This is the land of the troubadors and the mistral, of Cézanne and bull fights, of nightingales and war. For all its blood and scars and glory it is an innocent-looking land to drive through, flat and indolent, lonely and a touch scrubby. There are red poppies along the road, and cypresses, but mainly your eye is caught by the plane trees whose tops the French cut off in the first months of the year whenever they get around to it. Some of them look like the gnarled hands of old women, some are as stark and nude as telegraph poles; on others, topped back earlier, irrepressible new branches have begun to shoot straight upward from the ravaged trunks like thousands of long green candles. It is a mystic tree in a strange country.

It was raining again when we went through Aix-en-Provence but in Arles, only forty miles away, which you reach over roads that are as quiet as roads on the moon, there hadn't been any rain for six months. The air was clear and keen, like October air, and everything had a high, crystal sharpness and looked brand new. It was the same in Nîmes – where, under glass in the Maison Carrée, a handful of Americans have accomplished a curious kind of immortality. Show cases here contain a collection of Roman coins and an assortment of modern coins of various nations. There is a 1909 Lincoln penny, the gift, one is assured, of Mr. Herbert Claiborne Pill, Jr.; there is also a tiny gold California quarter presented on the 20th of October, 1903, by Mrs. Frederick F. Thompson, and a $3 gold piece of 1854, added to the collection by Daisy M. Orleman, M.D., in memory of her visit to Nîmes on the 17th of March, 1904.

In this region, in any season, you see the hurrying Hudsons and Lincolns of American tourists, intent on taking in, all in one day, Arles, Nîmes, Aigues-Mortes, Tarascon, the Saintes Maries, the Pont du Gard, the dead town of Les Baux, the bridge in Avignon, and the old church in St. Gilles. Americans have a strange inability to spot each other in a foreign land. I was frequently complimented on my English by ladies and gentlemen from Oregon, New Jersey, Virginia, and even Ohio. "You speak English very well," they invariably told me. "Ees because," I liked to reply, lapsing into my natural accent, "I am leeving for forty-three years in New York and Ohio." "Think of that," they always said. I didn't get to talk to the Clevelanders whose bright new car I saw in the ancient city under the Black Mountain but I imagine they would have been astonished at my accent. Their license plates bore the announcement of the 150th anniversary of the opening of the Northwest Territory. The proud boast looked a little pale inside the walls of Carcassonne and somehow reminded you of Shirley Temple cutting in on May Robson with an anecdote about the old days.

To get to Carcassonne – for I am ahead of myself – tourists usually go through Montpellier without stopping, but this can be a mistake. There was a tremendous street carnival going on when we reached there, the largest I have seen in France, with at least forty merry-go-rounds and similar dangerous contraptions and two or three unforgettable sideshows. On the painted canvas walls of one of these the Sirens of the Sea were advertised – first time in France, only fifty centimes to get in. Inside, in a tank six feet by four, and perhaps five feet deep, an enormous young woman with gold teeth splashed around in the water, wearing a faded blue bathing suit and a white rubber cap and wrestling with a snake perhaps four feet long which was either dead or, worn out by the unequal struggle, had fainted. In an adjoining tent, labeled Spectacle de New York, one was privileged for fifty centimes to gaze upon the various methods by which gangsters are punished in the jails of that cruel city: the electric chair, the iron maiden, and the Third Degree – which last proved to be an iron-spiked battleax. But what Montpellier will always bring to my mind first, I suppose, is an item I found in a copy of the London *Times* which I managed to buy there. "While the band was playing at the Changing of the Guard in the Grand Quadrangle of

Windsor Castle yesterday," the remarkable news story announced, "a pigeon settled on the bearskin of one of the guardsmen. The guardsman managed to shake it off, but it instantly flew onto the pack of another of the Guard, and refused to move until the Company Sergeant Major advanced upon it. It then flew away." An article in an adjoining column announced, with equal composure, that the army of General Franco had reached the sea.

From Carcassonne a road runs northwest through the *cassoulet* country to Toulouse, but for Luchon you take the southwest route, through the *paté de foie gras* country. Just outside the hamlet of Fanjeaux you see the Pyrenees for the first time, like clouds in the sky, white and still and far away. You couldn't reach them before lunch and the place to stop for that was the Hôtellerie Barbacane in Foix. The waiters were dressed in bright costumes of the region and one of them told us that he had fought side by side with the Americans for four months during the first World War. He also told us that the sporting way to get to the next town, St. Girons, was by way of a narrow mountain road, C 17, a route both *belle* and *sauvage*. We went along it till we came to two workmen who told us we couldn't get through without chains on account of the snow, so we turned around, a feat on C 17, and went back to the National Road that parallels the Pyrenees a little farther north. This road brought us to Montréjeau where we turned sharply south for Luchon and the Spanish border and rode toward one of the finest peaks of the range.

Hemingway has written that in the Spanish shadow of the Pyrenees, which Republican militiamen and civilians began to crawl out of in March by way of the Val d'Aran, military positions could be held by "determined graduates of any good girls' finishing school". It is interesting to note that in the first Catalonian campaign that threatened the stability of the world, twenty-one hundred and fifty-six years ago, the native tribes of the region held off the advance of the Carthaginian army for several months, destroyed a fourth of it, but finally let Hannibal fight through to the mountains. The tribesmen of 218 B.C. had been promised help from Rome (one of the fondest speculations of military historians is whether Hannibal could have battled his way from the Ebro to the Pyrenees against Roman legions). When help never came, the Catalonians of two thousand years ago probably felt as discouraged as the defenders of 1938 in the face of natural allies who seemed resigned to the triumph of Franco.

I had expected to have to wind and climb into Luchon but the road is straight and flat through the valley of a little stream called the Pique. All my expectations of Luchon turned out to be wrong. I had looked for crowds and turmoil but there was no rumor of either. The French papers had been full of the flight over the mountains of anywhere from four to eight thousand people. Special writers had been sending out from Luchon the conflicting, patchy, and excited stories that French journalists do on such occasions. It is twenty-five miles from Montréjeau into Luchon. A few sleepy white oxen were to be seen on the road, and girls on bicycles, and French soldiers wandering around in aimless groups of three or four. There was no sign of a refugee and no more feel of tension than you'd find in an apple orchard. The trees wore their new green, the Pique burbled merrily along, and the mountains were as cold and untroubled as stars.

A clock was striking seven when we drove into Luchon but it was still bright daylight. The town was quiet and almost empty, a resort out of season. There were only a few people on the long drowsy main street, a woman carrying a loaf of bread, a man trying to ride a bicycle and lead an unhappy calf at the same time, two army officers chatting and laughing. All the many hotels on this street except one were closed, and in the lobby of that one a single lonely figure moved slowly about. In a barber shop, the barbers lay relaxed in their chairs, one with a newspaper over his face, listening to a loud radio. In the doorway of a deserted *tabac* a girl watched the man and the calf with an unamused stare. A *couturière's* shop named "Mary Jane" and a bar called La Refuge slept behind their iron shutters. We drove around a big vacant square till we came to the hotel we had picked out in the *Michelin* guide – it had been marked "Open all year". Luchon had two seasons, winter and summer; in between times there was nothing going on; it was like an abandoned ballroom.

There was no sign of life about the big hotel, which consisted of two five-storey buildings joined together. I got out and tried one of the doors but couldn't open it. A little boy of about eight appeared briefly in another door and gave us a surprised look. We went through that door into a vast, cold, and gloomy lobby. It was obvious that there were no guests in the place and hadn't been for a long time. The day was fading, and the lobby seemed to get larger and darker and colder as we stood there. Parts of the gloom moved and they turned out to be an old woman and a younger woman. We found out that they ran the place. A porter silently detached himself from the darkness and brought in our bags. A chambermaid whose white cap moved like a cloud in the night led us up an enormous staircase to a big room that had been shuttered for months. She opened the shutters and went away and came back with some firewood and a vase of lilacs. The room got fairly warm after a while.

The man who had brought in our bags served dinner in our room at 8:30 having changed into freshly pressed waiter's clothes. I had peeked into the big dining room and it was as cold as a skating rink. The waiter said his name was François and that he was a Spaniard. François brought a map of Spain with the coffee and explained about the refugees. He said everything was so quiet because the border had been closed two days before; we had just missed the excitement. The French had handled the refugees with speed and competence. There weren't any more of them to be seen. Most of them had been put on trains to be sent back to Spain; the others were being taken care of in Toulouse, he thought, or somewhere. He had talked to some of the refugees as they came through; they were war-weary and discouraged. They said they had wandered around for weeks without seeing any officers. They had had enough.

François's bias was anti-leftist. He said that he did not belong to any party, he was not for either side, but what Spain needed was a Strong Hand. With Franco's victory there would come a Strong Hand. Mussolini and Hitler would have no say at all. Another hostile border for France? Nothing to worry about. Everything would be all right. There would be no Fascism – just a Strong Hand that would make everything fine. François talked like a lot of people you used to hear chattering at tea parties in Europe. Only a miracle could win for the Leftists, and there would be no miracle, said François.

The next morning was bright and clear, and we drove on toward the border until the road began to narrow and crawl up the mountain, and we couldn't go any farther. We drove back through Luchon, passing one or two ox carts groaning along at a mile an hour under heavy loads of tree trunks. It was high noon in Luchon, but the town was still asleep. We stopped for lunch in Tarbes, where our waiter spoke English with a fine American accent. He wasn't interested in what we had seen in Luchon or what had been going on there. What he wanted to know was whether the Brevoort Hotel still existed in New York. He said his father had been chef there twenty years before. We told him the Brevoort was fine.

From Tarbes it was an easy drive to Lourdes, the town of miracles, and around there we began to pick up tourists' cars again. It is interesting to find that *Michelin*, like François, does not believe in miracles, or anyway doesn't say anything about them. At the end of the information given about a town in the guidebook you often find a mention of its speciality. For Lourdes, it says: "*Specialité: Chocolat*".

7

AFTER CATO, WHAT?

It may be true that the trains run on schedule in Italy now, but the guards at grade crossings are not taking any chances. They run their gates down anywhere from fifteen to forty minutes before a train comes along. I have often smoked half a pack of cigarettes waiting for a train at a crossing. Ox carts and mule carts pile up despondently, but you do not see many cars. Gasoline costs nearly seventy cents a gallon in Italy and few Italians can afford to drive cars, even the little Fiats. This is fortunate, for Italians drive as if Hannibal were after them in a Duesenberg, and on crowded roads would soon kill each other off. The people of the European countries I have been in all drive wildly, but whereas the speed of the French grows out of a vivid impatience and that of the English out of a studied recklessness, the fury of the Italians seems to be born of an angry hysteria. Descending from a vehicle, an Italian sheds his frenzy like a cloak, puts on a thin but comfortable apathy, and stands about in the street.

The men of Italian towns and villages do not seem to do anything except stand in the street. Many of them stand quite still, others move around slightly. It is possible to drive through towns in Normandy and Brittany without seeing anybody, but the streets of Italian towns are almost impassable because of the men standing in them. In Grosseto one evening I decided to stand around with the men of the town to see if I could find out what there is in it. I moved around with those who were moving around and then stood for a while with those who were just standing. It seemed very dull, but perhaps I didn't keep at it long enough. This singular Italian habit is not a strange phenomenon of the present political regimentation, for it originated more than two thousand years ago. I quote from Theodor Mommsen's "History of Rome": "The habit of lounging was visibly on the increase. Cato the Elder proposed to have the market place paved with pointed stones in order to put a stop to the habit of idling; the Romans laughed at the jest and went on to enjoy the pleasure of loitering and gazing around them." After more than twenty centuries the Italians still love to loiter and gaze around them. I feel the same way about it that Cato did.

Cato the Elder is my favorite character in Italian history and I am glad that we have come to him so soon. He was fond of a little incantation which he believed would ward off sprains and he repeated it over and over whenever he felt a sprain coming on. Mommsen gives the "formula" for this potent in a footnote to his history and I am pleased to pass it on to you; whenever, then, you feel in danger of twisting a wrist or pulling a tendon you just keep saying, "Hauat hauat hauat ista pista sista damia bodannaustra." This is much simpler than another ancient Roman formula, for the prevention of gout, which I feel sure old Cato would never have had the patience to go through with. In practicing this gout formula, says Mommsen, you had to think of some other person, while fasting, and then repeat the incantation twenty-seven times, touching the earth each time and spitting. Cato, I like to believe, would have regarded that one as a lot of newfangled tomfoolery, as idle as standing in the street.

Cato regarded a great many things as tomfoolery, among them priests and women. His inquiry as to how a priest could meet another priest without laughing is still famous and has been attributed to everybody from Roger Bacon to H. L. Mencken. He declared that all women are plaguy and proud, and that if a man were quit of them he would lead a less godless life. He considered it a lot of damned nonsense and a major mistake on the part of the gods that women were so constituted as to play a necessary part in the perpetuation of the race. Gave them notions, made them think they were somebody. He wrote thousands of words denouncing women, practically all of them sound, but he had, unfortunately, no more effect on changing the morals of his day than D. H. Lawrence had on changing the morals of his. Indeed Cato lived to see women emancipated to a position of troublesome independence. They possessed property, they raised their voices in the home, a few of them poisoned their husbands, statues were erected to some of them here and there in Italy. Things reached, in short, that pretty pass where they have ever since remained.

Cato's own family life was conducted with disciplined authority but, in spite of everything, with no little tenderness. None of the women of his household every pushed him completely out of the supervision of any part of its activities. No child of his could be bathed and swaddled unless he was present or had given notice to the effect that he wouldn't be present. I have no doubt the old general could have changed an infant as well as anybody. I am sure he regarded women's pretensions to peculiar and mystic abilities in this connection as a lot of hokery-pokery. The line in all his writings which endears him to me most is that in which he set down, with stern dignity, the fact that none of his daughters ever caught him manifesting demonstrative affection toward his wife – except once, during a thunderstorm, when she was frightened. The old gentleman liked his food and his wine, and in his book on husbandry gives the recipe for his own pick-me-up for hangovers. He was wise enough to know that no chant is going to do you any good the morning after a bout with the wine cups. Hauat hauat hauat is just so much bodannaustra at a time like that, and he was probably the first to find it out. The fact that he believed up to the day of his death that you could ward off sprains by making a noise like an owl simply proves how human he was.★

★

I am convinced that if Cato were alive he would improve

★ Cf. Appendix, page 266

the system of transporting a motorcar by water from Naples to Genoa as it exists under the dread Heir of the Caesars. Nobody in Naples will tell you, to begin with, where the ship is. You have to hunt for it. This is to develop your sense of initiative and ingenuity. People who are told where ships are get soft. When you find the ship they don't want to let you on. A man discovers that you have no Italian visa. You explain that an American doesn't have to have an Italian visa. He points out that, nevertheless, you haven't got one. When you are finally allowed on board you are put in the wrong stateroom and are advised of this after you have unpacked your bags and lain down. This is to teach you to be ready for anything at any time. The purser then appears and takes your automobile papers away from you with an explanation similar to the undecipherable primitive Iapygian inscriptions that were found on the Calabrian peninsula. The last that you saw of the automobile itself it was drifting despondently out to sea on a large raft. If this does not teach you to have faith in the mysterious workings of a system you do not understand, nothing ever will.

In Genoa in the morning, you wait for two hours for your car to be put on the dock, although it was the only one on the ship. All the gasoline has been taken out of it and none is put back in. The purser has disappeared from your life forever with your papers. You find yourself in the midst of several hundred men standing or moving slowly around. It now becomes necessary to take all your bags and your tennis racquets out of the car and carry them into the customs house. You explain that your bags have already passed the customs at Ventimiglia and that you haven't been out of Italy since. The customs man gives the old sprain incantation and sticks a tiny stamp on each bag. A soldier in a gray cloak makes two small pencil marks on each stamp. After you have found your papers and got some *benzina* (it would take hours to tell how this is done) you pile all the bags in the car and drive ninety feet to a man who looks like the man who put the stamps on. He is not, however. He is the man who takes the stamps off. You haul all the bags out of the car and he removes the stamps one at a time. You pile the bags back in again and you are ready to go. Thus has the genius of Mussolini instilled energy and efficiency into maritime transportation facilities.

Mussolini (since we have arrived at him) has muscled into all the guidebooks in Rome, even those purporting to be devoted to the life and achievements of Appius Claudius and Augustus Caesar. Over the shoulder of every great consul and emperor, every painter and sculptor, peers the busy head of Benito the Magnificent, stealing the light of ancient glories. "Let us begin," says one of the guidebooks, "from the Capitol, the center and heart of the town's life, the majesty of which Michelangelo has expressed in terms of architecture, and which from the genius and love of Mussolini has received a new and still more solemn dignity." Whereupon the guide to Rome's treasures and antiquities degenerates into a preface to Mussolini. At the end of every guidebook in English one expects to see the famous lines of Browning, slightly changed by official order, "Open my heart, and you will see graven inside of it, 'Il Duce'." The Great Man has, of course, gone too far with his face. His elated subjects are incapable of snickering, but men cannot continue forever to cheer the utterly commonplace: the striking of a clock in a town of clocks, the falling of rain in a rainy land, a glowering familiar face on every wall and hoarding . In a movie theater in Rome during a newsreel the belligerent figure of the helmeted Dux striding across the screen, ripe for applause, was received in a complete silence. There was, to be sure, no disapproval in the silence, no hint of strain about it; it was simply devoid of any quality at all, like the eyes of a man looking out a train window. It may be because of the psychological necessity to laugh at some face or other that the heads of Laurel and Hardy are to be seen everywhere in Italy, running Il Duce a fairly close second. You find them on signboards, in movie lobbies, on the walls of buildings, as decorations on fancy stationery, in the form of figurines, ashtrays, toys, and *portafortunas*. It is, of course, too much to hope that the Italianos detect in *Signor* Hardy a certain resemblance to the Leader.

The *Saturday Evening Post* (to go on to something more interesting) costs fifty cents (ten lire) in Italy and *Photoplay* seventy-five cents. I have actually seen Americans carrying copies of them about, too. This is no doubt why the vendors of tortoise shell and camellias in the streets of Naples invariably approach an American with the chant "You millionaire, I broke, you millionaire, I broke." "It just happens," I told one of them, "that I saved less than four hundred thousand dollars out of the

Wall Street crash." He still insisted I was a millionaire. Nobody believes or pays much attention to anything an American or Englishman says in Italy. They are held in a kind of negligent contempt as the last millionaire representatives of a decadent and outmoded form of government destined to end up as a footnote to the history books of the totalitarian future. English and American books, newspapers, and magazines attacking Fascism you can buy anywhere. The issue of *Time* carrying a colored reproduction of Peter Blume's painting which presents the head of Mussolini as a jack-in-the-box was on sale at every kiosk in Rome for a week. "Ickes Attacks Fascism!" shouted the front page of the Paris *Herald-Tribune* from a rack in front of a store in the Piazza di Spagna. If it's writ in English it's writ in water, appears to be the official government attitude – if it has any attitude – toward the printed chatterings of the dying Democracies. On the bulletin board in the first-class lounge of the ship from Naples to Genoa appeared three separate copies of the day's wireless news in English. I took one of them as a souvenir. The leading story, under a Washington date line, began (I quote exactly) as follows, "In long awaited address to Congress Roosevelt plunged straight into international situation states *Daily Telegraph* correspondent and speech which broadcasted throughout world declared that dictatorships jeopardized civilization and world peace only safe in Democracies hands." A summary of the whole speech followed. I asked a steward who spoke English what he thought about it. He just laughed. So did I, perhaps a bit hollowly.

After Cato, What?

The sharpest impression that I brought out of Italy was a vivid mental image of the late Colonel Johnstone of the Fifth New York Cavalry, of all people. A certain tableau in which the Colonel became involved some seventy-five years ago was brought to my attention, amazingly enough, in the lounge of the Grand Hotel in Sorrento and for a time erased from my memory the fond picture of Cato the Elder embracing his wife during a thunderstorm. In this hotel lounge there was a bookcase holding perhaps the strangest assortment of English books to be found on the Continent, among them Harold MacGrath's "Man on the Box", Lilly Wesselhoeft's (I think it was Wesselhoeft) "Flipwing, the Spy", the New York Stock Exchange Investment Guide for 1912, and seven or eight enormous volumes containing the official reports of officers of the Federal Army and of the Army of the Confederate States of America on the various battles and campaigns of the War of the Rebellion. I took the volume entitled "Chancellorsville" to read after dinner one night. It contains, in addition to the complete records of that great battle, sundry accounts of less important engagements during the spring of 1863. Every now and then the exploits of Captain (later Major) John S. Mosby, the celebrated Rebel guerrilla leader, pop up. One report of his activities as set down by a Northern lieutenant I must give in full, for it bodies forth, in a brief and vivid frame of words, the deathless vignette of Colonel Johnstone of the Fifth New York Cavalry that so deeply affected me:

FAIRFAX COURT HOUSE, VA.
MARCH 9, 1863, 3.30 A.M.

GENERAL COMMANDING:

Captain Mosby, with his command, entered this town this morning at 2 A.M. They captured my patrols, horses, etc. They took Brigadier General Stoughton and horses, and all his men detached from his brigade. They took every horse they could find, public and private, and the commanding officer of the post, Colonel Johnstone of the Fifth New York Cavalry, made his escape from them in a nude state by accident. They searched for me in every direction but being on the Vienna Road, visiting outposts, I made my escape.

L. L. O'CONNOR,
Lieut.-Provost Marshal

My recollection of what the soldiers of the Duce look like has been somewhat obscured by this clear-cut picture of the confused hell that broke loose in Fairfax Court House on the morning of March 9, 1863. The eight million heirs of Caesar's Tenth Legion, who, with the armies of the Führer and the Mikado, may someday unite again Communism, Democracy, and the other powers of darkness in order to bring light and peace to an undisciplined world may be something to worry about. If so, you will have to worry about them. Italy and her boasts and threats have begun to fade from my mind. I keep thinking of Colonel Johnstone of the Fifth New York Cavalry. I can't help wondering what ever became of him.

8

THERE'S NO PLACE LIKE HOME

Idling through a London bookstore in the summer of 1937, I came upon a little book called "Collins' Pocket Interpreters: France". Written especially to instruct the English how to speak French in the train, the hotel, the quandary, the dilemma, etc, it is, of course, equally useful – I might also say equally depressing – to Americans. I have come across a number of these helps-for-travellers, but none that has the heavy impact, the dark, cumulative power of Collins'. A writer in a London magazine mentions a phrase book got out in the era of Imperial Russia which contained this one magnificent line: "Oh, dear, our postillion has been struck by lightning!" but that fantastic piece of disaster, while charming and provocative – though, I daresay, quite rare even in the days of the Czars – is to Mr. Collins' modern, workaday disasters as Fragonard is to George Bellows, or Sarah Orne Jewett to William Faulkner. Let us turn the pages of this appalling little volume.

Each page has a list of English expressions one under the other, which gives them the form of verse. The French translations are run alongside. Thus, on the first page, under "The Port of Arrival," we begin (quietly enough) with "Porter, here is my baggage!" – "*Porteur, voici mes bagages!*" From then on disaster follows fast and follows faster until in the end, as you shall see, all hell breaks loose. The volume contains three times as many expressions to use when one is in trouble as when everything is going all right. This, my own experience has shown, is about the right ratio, but God spare me from some of the difficulties for which the traveller is prepared in Mr. Collins' melancholy narrative poem. I am going to leave out the French translations because, for one thing, people who get involved in the messes and tangles we are coming to invariably forget their French and scream in English anyway. Furthermore, the French would interrupt the fine, free flow of the English and spoil what amounts to a dramatic tragedy of overwhelming and original kind. The phrases, as I have said, run one under the other, but herein I shall have to run them one after the other (you can copy them down the other way, if you want to).

Trouble really starts in the canto called "In the Customs Shed". Here we have: "I cannot open my case." "I have lost my keys." "Help me to close this case." "I did not know that I had to pay." "I don't want to pay so much." "I cannot find my porter." "Have you seen porter 153?" That last query is a little master stroke of writing, I think, for in those few words we have a graphic picture of a tourist lost in a jumble of thousands of bags and scores of customs men, looking frantically for one of at least a hundred and fifty-three porters. We feel that the tourist will not find porter 153, and the note of frustration has been struck.

Our tourist (accompanied by his wife, I like to think) finally gets on the train for Paris – having lost his keys and not having found his porter – and it comes time presently to go to the dining car, although he probably has no appetite, for the customs men, of course, have had to break open that one suitcase. Now, I think, it is the wife who begins to crumble: "Someone has taken my seat." "Excuse me, sir, that seat is mine." "I cannot find my ticket!" "I have left my ticket in the compartment." "I will go and look for it." "I have left my gloves (my purse) in the dining car." Here the note of frenzied disintegration, so familiar to all travellers abroad, is sounded. Next comes "The Sleeper", which begins, ominously, with "What is the matter?" and ends with "May I open the window?" "Can you open this window, please?" We realize, of course, that *nobody* is going to be able to open the window and that the tourist and his wife will suffocate. In this condition they arrive in Paris, and the scene there, on the crowded station platform, is done with superb economy of line: "I have left something in the train." "A parcel, an overcoat." "A mackintosh, a stick." "An umbrella, a camera." "A fur, a suitcase." The travellers have now begun to go completely to pieces, in the grand manner.

Next comes an effective little interlude about an airplane trip, which is one of my favorite passages in this swift and sorrowful tragedy: "I want to reserve a place in the plane leaving tomorrow morning." "When do we start?" "Can we get anything to eat on board?" "When do we arrive?" "I feel sick." "Have you any paper bags for air-sickness?" "The noise is terrible." "Have you any cotton wool?" "When are we going to land?" This brief masterpiece caused me to cancel an air trip from London to Paris and go the easy way, across the Channel.

We now come to a section called "At the Hotel", in which things go from worse to awful: "Did you not get my letter?" "I wrote to you three weeks ago." "I asked for a first-floor room." "If you can't give me something better, I shall go away." "The chambermaid never comes when I ring." "I cannot sleep at night, there is so much noise." "I have just had a wire. I must leave at once." Panic has begun to set in, and it is not appeased any by the advent of "The Chambermaid": "Are you the chambermaid?" "There are no towels here." "The sheets on this bed are damp." "This room is not clean." "I have seen a mouse in the room." "You will have to set a mouse trap here." The bells of hell at this point begin to ring in earnest: "These shoes are not mine." "I put my shoes here, where are they now?" "The light is not good." "The bulb is broken." "The radiator is too warm." "The radiator doesn't work." "It is cold in this room." "This is not clean, bring me another." "I don't like this." "I can't eat this. Take it away!"

I somehow now see the tourist's wife stalking angrily out of the hotel, to get away from it all (without any shoes on), and, properly enough, the booklet seems to follow her course – first under "Guides and Interpreters": "You are asking too much." "I will not give you any more." "I shall call a policeman." "He can settle this affair." Then under "Inquiring the Way": "I am lost." "I was looking for – " "Someone robbed me." "That man robbed me." "That man is following me everywhere." She rushes to "The Hairdresser", where, for a change, everything goes quite smoothly until: "The water is too hot, you are scalding me!" Then she goes shopping, but there is no surcease: "You have not given me the right change." "I bought this two days ago." "It doesn't work." "It is broken." "It is torn." "It doesn't fit me." Then to a restaurant for a snack and a reviving cup of tea: "This is not fresh." "This piece is too fat." "This doesn't smell very nice." "There is a mistake in the bill." "While I was dining someone has taken my purse." "I have left my glasses (my watch) (a ring) in the lavatory." Madness has now come upon her and she rushes wildly out into the street. Her husband, I think, has at the same time plunged blindly out of the hotel to find her. We come then, quite naturally, to "Accident", which is calculated to keep the faint of heart – nay, the heart of oak – safely at home by his own fireside: "There has been an accident!" "Go and fetch a policeman quickly." "Is there a doctor near here?" "Send for the ambulance." "He is seriously injured." "She has been run over." "He has been knocked down." "Someone has fallen in the water." "The ankle, the arm." "The back, a bone." "The face, the finger." "The foot, the head." "The knee, the leg." "The neck, the nose." "The wrist, the shoulder." "He has broken his arm." "He has broken his leg." "He has a sprained ankle." "He has a sprained wrist." "He is losing blood." "He has fainted." "He has lost consciousness." "He has burnt his face." "It is swollen." "It is bleeding." "Bring some cold water." "Help me to carry him." (Apparently, you just let *her* lie there while you attend to him – but, of course, she was merely run over, whereas he has taken a terrific tossing around.)

We next see the husband and wife back in their room at the dreary hotel, both in bed, and both obviously hysterical. This scene is entitled "Illness": "I am feeling very ill, send for the doctor." "I have pains in – " "I have pains all over." "The back, the chest." "The ear, the head." "The eyes, the heart." "The joints, the kidneys." "The lungs, the stomach." "The throat, the tongue." "Put out your tongue." "The heart is affected." "I feel a pain here." "He is not sleeping well." "He cannot eat." "My stomach is out of order." "She is feverish." "I have caught a cold." "I have caught a chill." "He has a temperature." "I have a cough." "Will you give me a prescription?" "What must I do?" "Must I stay in bed?" "I feel better." "When will you come and see me again?" "Billiousness, rheumatism." "Insomnia, sunstroke." "Fainting, a fit." "Hoarseness, sore throat." "The medicine, the remedy." "A poultice, a draught." "A tablespoonful, a teaspoonful." "A sticking plaster, senna." "Iodine." That last suicidal bleat for iodine is, to me, a masterful touch.

Our couple finally get on their feet again, for travellers are tough – they've got to be – but we see under the next heading, "Common Words and Phrases", that they are left forever punch-drunk and shattered: "Can I help you?" "Excuse me." "Carry on!" "Look here!" "Look down there!" "Look up there!" "Why, how?" "When, where?" "Because." "That's it!" "It is too much, it is too dear." "It is very cheap." "Who, what, which?" "Look out!" Those are Valkyries, one feels, riding around, and above, and under our unhappy husband and wife. The book sweeps on to a mad operatic ending of the tragedy, with all the strings and brasses and wood winds going full blast: "Where are we going?" "Where are you going?" "Come quickly and see!" "I shall call a policeman." "Bring a policeman!" "I shall stay here." "Will you help me?" "Help! Fire!" "Who are you?" "I don't know you." "I don't want to speak to you." "Leave me alone." "That will do." "You are mistaken." "It was not I." "I didn't do it." "I will give you nothing." "Go away now!" "It has nothing to do with me." "Where should one apply?" "What must I do?" "What have I done?" "I have done nothing." "I have already paid you." "I have paid you enough." "Let me pass!" "Where is the British consulate?" The oboes take that last, despairing wail, and the curtain comes down.

APPENDIX

This under-developed snapshot of Cato, which catches him in a not unbecoming light, I found in the pages of Mommsen's "History of Rome" when I was in Italy five years ago. At that time and in that place, almost any ancient Roman was bound to seem to me an admirable and amusing fellow by comparison with the Fascist Dictator, old Stab-in-the-Back. There is a well-rounded portrait of Cato in Plutarch's "Lives" and a full-length painting, done in burning oils, in H. G. Wells's "Outline of History". For the sins of Marcus Porcius Cato were dark and manifold. He abandoned in Spain the war horse which had carried him to triumph there; he sold his slaves when they became old; he practiced usury on a grand scale. During his ten years of office as Censor, Cato interfered with the pastimes, pleasures and privileges of practically everyone in Rome except himself. He shook his little fist at the philosophy and culture of Greece, and persecuted her teachers. It was mainly because of him that the land on which Carthage once had stood was plowed up and sown with salt.

I have reprinted "After Cato, What?" in this book partly because the piece also contains a glimpse of Colonel Johnstone of the Fifth New York Cavalry flitting through the soft darkness of a Virginia night in the Year of Our Lord 1863. I didn't want to leave that out of this collection, for it is one of my favorite moments in history. Shortly after the story appeared in *The New Yorker*, seven or eight Southerners wrote me – one of them from Fairfax Court House – to report what had actually happened to Colonel Johnstone on that night. It seems that he concealed himself, with great ingenuity and the highest kind of courage, under the seat of an outside toilet, where he remained until Mosby and his men had gone. Thereupon he emerged, surely one of the most remarkable figures of the War between the States.